Documents on British
Economic and Social History
Book I   1750–1870

BRITAIN BECOMES
THE WORKSHOP OF THE WORLD

DOCUMENTS ON BRITISH
ECONOMIC AND SOCIAL HISTORY

Book One 1750–1870
Book Two 1870–1939
Book Three 1945–67

The aim of these books is to provide pupils in secondary schools with a full survey of the developments in British economic and social life since 1750.

Documents on British Economic and Social History

Book One 1750–1870

PETER LANE

HEAD OF THE HISTORY DEPARTMENT
COLOMA COLLEGE, WEST WICKHAM, KENT

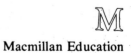
Macmillan Education

First edition 1968
Reprinted 1970, 1971, 1972, 1973, 1975, 1978 (twice), 1980

Published by
MACMILLAN EDUCATION LTD
*Houndmills Basingstoke Hampshire RG21 2XS
and London
Associated companies in Delhi Dublin
Hong Kong Johannesburg Lagos Melbourne
New York Singapore and Tokyo*

Printed in Hong Kong

The editor and publishers wish to state that the language of some of
the more obscure documents has been adapted to help the modern
reader, but they have been scrupulously anxious not to distort the
original meaning of the document.
The questions sometimes need more knowledge than the documents
alone can give. It is hoped that this will encourage research.
The editor wishes to thank Mr. W. J. Fowler for his very helpful sug-
gestions.

Contents

Acknowledgements

The publishers wish to thank the following for kind permission to reproduce the illustrations on the pages quoted: Aerofilms: 38, 39; British Museum: 111; Cambridge University Press: 14 (lower), from *Population Problems of the Age of Malthus* by G. Talbot Griffith; City of Birmingham Water Department: 88 (lower); City of Liverpool: 88 (upper); Clarendon Press, Oxford: 8 (upper), from *Living and Working* by L. F. Hobley; Greater London Council: 118 (lower); *Illustrated London News*: 68 (upper); Mansell Collection: 31, 48 (3), 68 (lower), 121; Methuen and Company: 28 (lower), 40, from *The Common People* by Cole and Postgate; National Buildings Record: 67; National Coal Board: 49; National Union of Agricultural Workers: 78 (lower); Newton Chambers and Company: 18 (lower); *Punch*: 98 (lower); Radio Times Hulton Picture Library: 28 (upper), 35, 47, 57, 58 (2), 65, 75, 98 (upper), 108 (lower), 113; J. K. St. Joseph: 108 (upper); Science Museum: 18 (upper); T. G. Warburton: 45; Textile Council, Manchester: 8 (lower); *The Times*: 118 (upper); Transport and General Workers Union: 78 (upper).

Comment

Plate 1a In the 'domestic' system, the family would work on material brought to the cottage by a merchant. The machinery was small enough to be used in a cottage, and was driven by hand.

Plate 1b The new spinning machines were far too big to be used in the cottage, and were driven by steam power, so that factories had to be built, and the cottage industry died out.

Children had helped in the cottage; the boy in Plate 1a is having a rest. Few people thought it wrong that they should work in the factory (Plate 1b). The baby brought up in the noise and dirt of the cottage would be as likely to be sickly as the child in the factory town, whose home did not house machines.

Questions

a. How many machines are in the cottage? How were they driven?
b. The father works a handloom, the baby is asleep in the same room. How would this affect the health of the child?
c. Who decided the hours of work in the cottage?
d. The spinning machine (Plate 1b) is in a cotton mill. Why could this machine not be housed in the cottages?
e. How does Plate 1b help you to understand: (*a*) the increased output, (*b*) the danger to life, of the factory system?

1a. Weaving in a cottage on a hand loom with a flying shuttle. In the background is a spinning jenny.

1b. The interior of a cloth mill, about 1840

1 The Domestic System for Manufacturing Woollen Cloth, 1724

. . . Two things essential to the [cloth industry] are found here . . . I mean Coals, and running Water upon the Tops of the highest Hills: . . . After we had mounted the third Hill, we found one continued Village, . . . hardly a House standing out of a speaking distance from another . . . We could see that at almost every House there was a Tenter [a frame for stretching cloth], and almost on every Tenter a Piece of Cloth . . . yet look which Way we would, high to the Tops, and low to the Bottoms, it was all the same; innumerable Houses and Tenters, and a white Piece upon every Tenter.

. . . I found . . . wherever we pass'd any House we found a little Gutter of running Water . . . At every considerable House was a Manufactury or Work-House . . . [and] the little Streams were so . . . guided by Gutters or Pipes . . . that none of those Houses were without a River . . . running into and through their Work-Houses . . .

Having thus Fire and Water at every Dwelling, there is no need to enquire why they dwell thus dispers'd upon the highest Hills, the Convenience of the Manufactures requiring it. Among the Manufacturers Houses are likewise scattered an infinite Number of Cottages or small Dwellings, in which dwell the Workmen which are employed, the Women and Children of whom are always busy Carding, Spinning, etc., so that no Hands being unemploy'd, all can gain their Bread, even from the youngest to the ancient; hardly any thing above four Years old, but its Hands are sufficient to it self.

Daniel Defoe, *A Tour thro' the whole Island of Great Britain*, vol. 1, 1724.

Comment

This extract describes the woollen industry around Halifax in Yorkshire in 1724, about forty years before the date usually given for the
beginning of the Industrial Revolution. Here there were many skilled
workers making, maintaining or operating machinery and practising
various crafts, such as engineering, weaving, spinning, dyeing: men who
were used to trading. These 'capitalists' were already in the woollen
industry at Halifax, and also in other industries in other parts of the
country.

The woollen industry was slower to adopt new machines than was the
newer cotton industry; there were plenty of skilled workers in wool and
more conservative producers. Also, it proved more difficult to design
machinery for the woollen threads than for the cotton. (See Document
5.)

Questions

a. What two things were essential to the woollen industry?
b. What was found outside every house? What was it used for? What is
 the meaning of 'on tenterhooks'?
c. Why did the people live on 'the highest hills'?
d. What work was done in the smallest cottages? (See also Plate 1a.)
e. At what age did children begin to work?
f. What evidence is there in this extract of: (i) fairly large-scale employers; (ii) the use of power to drive machinery?
g. Why did the cotton industry adopt machinery more readily than did
 the woollen industry? (See also Documents 5 and 8.)
h. What evidence is there in this extract that there were many skilled
 workpeople in Yorkshire in 1724?

2 Agriculture in Norfolk, 1771

... to give a slight review of the husbandry which has rendered the name of this county so famous in the farming world ... Great improvements have been made by means of the following:

FIRST: By inclosing.
SECOND: By a spirited use of marl (powdered rock and lime) and clay.
THIRD: By the introduction of an excellent rotation of crops.
FOURTH: By the culture of turnips well hand-hoed.
FIFTH: By the culture of clover and ray-grass.
SIXTH: By landlords granting long leases.
SEVENTH: By the county being divided chiefly into large farms.

... Take any one from the seven, and the improvement of Norfolk would never have existed ...

After the best managed inclosure, and the most spirited conduct in marling, still the whole success of the undertaking depends on this point: no fortune will be made in Norfolk by farming unless a judicious rotation of crops be pursued. That which has been chiefly adopted by the Norfolk farmers is:

1. Turnips; 2. Barley; 3. Clover; or clover and ray-grass; 4. Wheat.

... In the above rotation, the turnips are (if possible) manured and much of the wheat the same. This is a noble system, which keeps the soil rich; one exhausting crop is followed by a cleansing and ameliorating one. ...

If the preceding points are properly reviewed, it will at once be apparent that no small farmer would effect such great things as have been done in Norfolk. Inclosing, marling, and keeping a stock of sheep large enough for folding, belong absolutely and exclusively to great farmers. ... Split them into tenures of an hundred pounds a year, you will find nothing but beggars and weeds in the whole county.

Arthur Young, *The Farmer's Tour through the East of England*, 1771.

Comment

Young has two claims to a place in the history books. He reports what he saw, so that we know what England was like; and he told his contemporaries, so that farmers in the rest of the country learned about Norfolk farming.

Questions

a. Why was Norfolk famous in the farming world?
b. Give four changes in *farming methods* which Young said led to 'great improvements'.
c. What was meant by inclosure? Why did it result in 'large farms'?
d. What was the advantage of the new rotation system?
e. Why could 'no small farmer effect such things'?
f. How did the introduction of turnips help the dairy farmer?
g. Show that these improvements resulted in: (i) more fresh meat; (ii) more vegetables. How did these affect the health of the population?
h. How did Young help to spread knowledge of farming improvements?

3 Eighteenth-century Population Calculations, 1801

This is not a strictly contemporary document, since Rickman's calculations were based on the 1801 Census; but it is the only near-contemporary estimate and gives some idea of population trends in the 18th century. . . . [John Rickman (1771–1840) prepared the first Census Act of 1800, worked out the methods to be used and prepared the Census Reports of 1801, 1811, 1821 and 1831.]

TABLE of POPULATION throughout the last Century
ENGLAND AND WALES

In the Year	Population	In the Year	Population
1700	5,475,000	1770	7,428,000
1710	5,240,000	1780	7,953,000
1720	5,565,000	1785	8,016,000
1730	5,796,000	1790	8,675,000
1740	6,064,000	1795	9,055,000
1750	6,467,000	1801	9,168,000
1760	6,736,000		

John Rickman, *Eighteenth Century Population Calculations*, 1801.

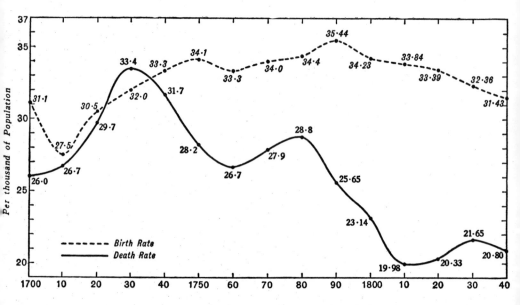

1c. Changes in the birth-rate and the death-rate from 1700 to 1840

Comment

The figures given here are only estimated, based on the figures from selected parish records on births, marriages and deaths. There can only be estimates, since there was no official Registrar of Births, Marriages and Deaths until 1837.

This increased population had to be fed, clothed and housed. The Agrarian Revolution provided the food, and the Industrial Revolution the clothing and houses, while a Transport Revolution was required to move the extra food, the raw materials and the manufactured goods.

Questions

a. By how much had the population grown between 1740 and 1795?

b. What percentage increase had taken place between 1740 and 1795?

c. Why was there a need for 50% more output in 1801 as compared with 1750?

d. Look at the graph. Was the increase in population due to a change in the birth-rate or death-rate? Give some reasons for the change.

e. 35·4 children were born in 1790 for every 1,000 people alive. How many children were born in that year? In 1800?

f. How many people died in 1730? In 1800?

g. When was the first official census taken? Can you suggest how Rickman used church records to help him make his estimates?

h. Give three reasons for the fall in the death-rate.

4 Tin-mining in Cornwall, 1750

. . . There are to each mine two shafts. . . . One they call the ladder-shaft, in which the perpendicular ladders are fixed . . .; (they are about thirty feet long). . . . The other is called the wem-shaft, from the wem or windlace,[1] turned by a horse, by the help of which they let down the tub, called a kible, to bring up the ore . . . Below the ladders, when they have come to the lode or vein, they burrow down in holes which they call gunnies. . . . Besides these shafts there is the fire engine shaft, by which they pump up the water by means of the engine, which was invented about forty or fifty years ago by Mr. Newcomen, of Dartmouth, and Captain Savory. At the bottom is a hole, about six feet deep, to receive the water which runs from all parts; . . . the water is pumped up 24 fathoms to the channel call'd an audit, which conveys it [away]; this audit is about thirty fathoms from the top, the whole being about 55 fathoms, or 330 feet. The lode or vein of tin (or copper) may be of a different thickness to twelve feet, and they call it a big or a small lode. . . . A succession of men are always in the mine, except on Sundays. They work eight hours, from six to two, and from two to ten, and from ten to six, and are out of the mine sixteen hours. When they come up, they call it coming to the grass. When the ore is brought up, women and children are employed in breaking it, and separating the [waste] from the ore, and the tin from the copper. . . . In the mines in general the lord has a fifteenth [share], and the owner, called the bounder, has a tenth.

[1] windlace = windlass.

Dr. Richard Pocock's description, 1750.

1d. A contemporary diagram of a Cornish copper mine in 1778. It has many of the features described in the text opposite.
O Wems
Q Water engine wheels
S Water engine bobs

(From Pryce: *Mineralogię Cornubiensis*)

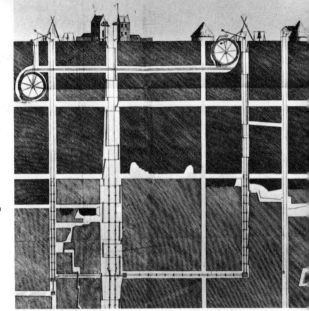

Comment

Some industries require little or no capital. Some modern ones require a huge capital outlay: in this extract is an example of capitalism in tin mining. Other industries requiring capital were coal, engineering, iron and shipbuilding.

The Industrial Revolution meant that factories became bigger (Plate 1*b*) and more numerous, and the need for extra capital arose.

Questions

a. Why did the mine have two shafts?

b. How was the ore brought up?

c. What invention was the work of Newcomen? Why was it necessary to pump up the water?

d. Why did the owner require a 'succession of men'? What were their hours of work?

e. Draw a sketch of the mine showing: (i) the depth at which water collected; (ii) the height to which it was pumped; (iii) how it was taken away.

f. How far down was the tin? How thick was it?

g. What evidence is there that heavy expenses would have to be met before any tin or copper was sold?

h. What work was done at the surface? Who did this work?

Comment

The steam engine was first used as an engine which would pump water out of the deeper mines (Documents 4 and 6). Several people played a part in the development of an improved engine. Savory and Newcomen (Document 4) had built one as well. James Watt's engine was an improvement on theirs.

That these engines were built proves that in England in the early 18th century there were a number of scientists, engineers, craftsmen, such as millwrights, and workshops: the Industrial Revolution could not have taken place without them.

Plate 2b: illustrating: (i) the normal siting of an early factory; (ii) that some factories were built near canals.

Questions

a. This machine (Plate 2a) was built in 1788. How does it prove the existence of skilled workers?
b. Watt improved on the work of Newcomen (Document 4). How does this help you to understand the term 'Industrial Revolution'?
c. How did the machine lead to an increased demand for coal?
d. Machinery had been driven by hand power (Plate 1a) and by water power (Document 5). Why would the steam engine be: (i) more productive than hand power; (ii) more dependable than water power?
e. The steam engine led to the building of factories. Why? Why were many factories built near canals?

2a. Boulton and Watt's rotative beam lap engine, 1788. It is one of the earliest examples of the double-acting rotative beam engine with separate condenser and air pump. It was known as the lap engine because it drove machinery which lapped or polished steel ornaments. It was a ten horsepower engine and was used at the Soho Manufactory near Birmingham till 1858.

2b. The Thorncliffe ironworks near Sheffield, from a painting dated 1811

5 The Introduction of Machinery into the Manchester Cotton Industry, 1783

. . . large exports for foreign trade [and] the interior business of the country is [such that] no exertion . . . [by] workmen could have answered the demands without the introduction of spinning machines. . . . People saw children from nine to twelve years of age manage these machines with dexterity and bring plenty into families that were before overburdened with children.

The weavers were afraid [that] the manufacturers would demand finer weft woven at the former prices, which occasioned some risings; and the 'jennies' were opposed, some being demolished before those who used them could . . . convince others of their general utility. [At last] Dorning Rasbotham, Esq., a worthy magistrate, convinced the weavers . . . that it was their true interest to encourage 'jennies'.

The improvements kept increasing till the capital engines for twist were perfected; and it is amazing to see what thousands of spindles may be put in motion by a water wheel.

When the larger machines were first set to work by water, they soon outrivalled the making of warps on the larger 'jennies'. . . .

We gave in our [original] manuscript a particular description of the principles and movements of these machines; but have suppressed it for the present, as it has been hinted that this publication may be translated into French and communicated to our rivals in trade.

Nothing has more contributed to the improvements in trade here than the free admission of workmen . . . whereby the trade has been kept open to strangers of every description who contribute to its improvement by their ingenuity; for Manchester being only a market town, governed by Constables, is not subject to such regulations as are made in corporations[1] to favour freemen to the exclusion of strangers.

[1] A corporate town was one which had received a Royal Charter, and had a corporation and Mayor and Councillors. These often made laws which prevented 'strangers' (i.e. non citizens of the town) setting up in business.

James Ogden, *A description of Manchester*, 1783.

Comment

This document was written by James Ogden, a Manchester school-master and poet, and it tells of the changes that had taken place in the Manchester cotton industry by 1783. This industry was a new one but growing for the reasons given in the first lines of the document.

The restrictive regulations referred to in the last paragraph hampered the growth of the woollen industry, which was to take second place to cotton in the 19th century. (Document 1.)

Questions

a. What two reasons does Ogden give to explain the need for machinery?
   How does the evidence of Document 3 support this?
b. Children worked the first machines. Why did parents welcome this?
c. Who opposed the introduction of spinning jennies? Why?
d. Why did jennies result in higher wages for the weavers?
e. The larger machines were first set to work by water. What power had
   been used before? What would be used later?
f. Who were our rivals in trade in 1783? Name two colonies where this
   rivalry had led to war.
g. Name three methods of driving machinery. (See also Plates 1a and
   b.) How does this help to explain the rise of the Lancashire cotton
   industry?
h. What was one difference between 'a town governed by constables'
   and 'a corporation'? How does this difference help to explain the
   rise of the Lancashire cotton industry?

6 The State of the Coal Trade, 1829

What is the deepest pit you know? — The deepest pit I am acquainted with as a working pit is 180 fathoms of shaft; but they frequently go deeper.

Can you state generally what is the extent of the expense incurred in sinking a single pit? — I have known several cases upwards of £30,000; that includes the machinery for sinking that pit, the steam engine and all its apparatus; that is merely getting to the coal, and it might be called more properly a winning charge than a working charge. I should think that the aggregate capital employed by coal owners on the river Tyne must amount to about a million and a half, exclusive of craft in the river.

Have you any calculations of the number of men and ships employed on the two rivers (Tyne and Wear)? — I have made a summary; there are, seamen 15,000, pitmen and above ground people employed at the collieries 21,000, keelmen, coal boatmen, casters and trimmers 2,000, making the total number employed in what I call the Northern coal trade, 38,000.

Do you think that the particular accidents by explosions, which you have described, have been much lessened by the introduction of Sir Humphrey Davy's safety lamp? — They have, I conceive. If we had not had the Davy lamp, these mines could not now have been in existence at all; for the only substitute we had, and that was not a safe one, was what we called steel mills. They were completely superseded by the Davy lamp of the simplest construction; it costs only about 5 or 6 shillings. A steel mill is very hard work; we were obliged to have two persons to relieve each other; and this lamp was introduced in its room: . . . this introduced quite a new era in coal mining, as many collieries are now in existence, and old collieries have been reopened, producing the best coals, which must have lain dormant but for the introduction of the Davy lamp.

Evidence of J. Buddle before the Select Committee of the House of Lords on the state of the coal trade, 1829.

Comment

The coal trade was an old one — it flourished in Newcastle in the 15th century. The demand for coal increased in the late 18th and 19th centuries, with its use in the iron industry (Document 7), the growing engineering industry and for producing steam power in the textile industries.

The capitalist nature of industry (Document 4) is illustrated here. £30,000 was a vast amount of money when you think that Kay's flying shuttle cost £6 to buy and Davy's lamp only 5s. Davy's lamp is discussed in the document — we can see how important it was to the safety of the miners, and how it helped to make it possible to develop deeper mines.

Questions

a. Look at Document 4 again. How many feet make a fathom? How deep was the 'deepest mine'?
b. What problems would a deep mine present? (Think of Davy, Newcomen and winding gear.)
c. Why was the coal industry a capitalistic industry?
d. How much did the Davy lamp cost? What light had been used previously?
e. In what ways was the Davy lamp an improvement?
f. How does the extract show that the demand for coal was increasing?
g. How did coal decide the location of industry? (See also Plate 4a.)
h. Show how (i) local landowners, (ii) country banks, (iii) rich merchants helped in the development of local industries. (See last sentence of Document 4.)

7 A Letter Describing Developments in Ironworks, *c.* 1783

It was my Husband's Father that attempted to mould and cast Iron pots, etc., in sand instead of Loam in which he succeeded at an Air Furnace in Bristol. About the year 1709 he came into Shropshire to Coalbrookdale. He here cast Iron Goods in sand out of the Blast Furnace that blow'd with wood charcoal. Sometime after he suggested the thought that it might be practable [*sic*] to smelt the Iron from the ore in the blast Furnace with Pit Coal. He first try'd with raw coal as it came out of the Mines, but it did not answer. He, not discouraged, had the coal coak'd into Cynder, as is done for drying Malt, and it then succeeded to his satisfaction.

My Husband Abraham Darby was but Six years old when his Father died, but he inherited his genius, enlarg'd upon his plan, and made many improvements. . . .

About 26 years ago my Husband conceived this happy thought, that it might be possible to make iron bar from pit-coal pigs. A good account being given of their working, he erected Blast Furnaces for Pig Iron for Forges.

Had not these discoveries been made the Iron trade of our own produce would have dwindled away, for woods for charcoal became very Scarce and landed Gentlemen [raised] the prices of wood exceeding high.

Many other improvements he was the author of. He got roads made and laid with Sleepers and rails and brings them to the Furnaces in Waggons. And one waggon with three horses will bring as much as twenty horses used to bring on horses' backs. Of late years the laying of the rails of cast Iron was substituted; which, altho' expensive, answers well for [wear] and Duration.

Letter from Mrs. Darby, *circa* 1783.

Comment

Professor Ashton has pointed out that this letter makes it clear that it was the first Abraham Darby, not his son, who first used coke in place of charcoal in the production of iron castings. This substitution of coke for charcoal meant that the iron industry moved from the woodlands of Gloucester, Sussex and other old centres to the coal-fields of the Midlands, Yorkshire and South Wales (Document 6).

If you think about the machinery that was used in industry, the bridges, railway engines and lines, and the wider use of metals, you will see that without the revolution in the iron industry there would have been little chance of a revolution in other fields.

Questions

a. When did Abraham Darby's father begin his experiments? Look up the date for Newcomen's invention (Document 4).
b. What fuel did he use at first? Why did this mean that the iron industry would not have developed very much?
c. What fuel did he fail with? What did he succeed with?
d. Why did the Darbys' success mean: (i) a reduction in the income of some landed gentlemen; (ii) an increased demand for coal? (See Document 6.)
e. How did Darby take the coal and iron to his furnaces?
f. Why were 'rail and horse' cheaper and quicker than horse pack? (See Plate 3.)
g. Use the names of (i) Savory, Newcomen and Watt, (ii) the Darbys and Cort to show that changes in industry took place over a long period of time.
h. Show that the changes in the iron industry helped: (i) the production of machinery; (ii) the changes in transport.

8 The Declaration of the Framework Knitters, 1812

By the charter granted by our late sovereign Lord, Charles II, the framework knitters are empowered to break and destroy all frames and engines that fabricate articles in a fraudulent and deceitful manner, and to destroy all framework knitters' goods whatsoever that are so made. An Act passed in the 28th year of our present sovereign Lord George III enacted that persons entering by force into any house, shop or place to break or destroy frames should be adjudged guilty of felony. We are fully convinced that such Act was obtained in the most fraudulent manner; we therefore, the framework knitters, do hereby declare the aforesaid Act to be null and void. And we do hereby declare to all hosiers, lace manufacturers and proprietors of frames that we will break and destroy all manner of frames whatsoever that make the following spurious articles and all frames whatsoever that do not pay the regular prices heretofore agreed to [by] the masters and workmen . . . and all frames of whatsoever description the workmen of whom are not paid in the current coin of the realm will invariably be destroyed . . .

Given under my hand this first day of January, 1812 at Ned Lud's Office, Sherwood Forest.

Public Records Office, Home Office.

Comment

The Luddite Riots of 1811–12 began in Nottinghamshire, where the hosiery workers objected not to the use of new machinery but to certain trade practices by the employers. The Yorkshire riots, on the other hand, were directed chiefly against the introduction of cloth dressing machinery (Document 5).

Questions

a. Why did the Act of Charles II allow framework knitters to destroy frames and engines?

b. How might this Act have prevented the introduction of new machinery?

c. Why had the Act of George III been passed?

d. What evidence is there that trade, industry and prices were regulated by the State in the 18th century?

e. What did the Luddites think of the Act of George III? Why?

f. What did they intend to do to the new machinery? Why?

g. What evidence is there that new machinery led to lower wages for some people?

h. What action did the Government take against the Luddites?

3a. A pack-horse convoy

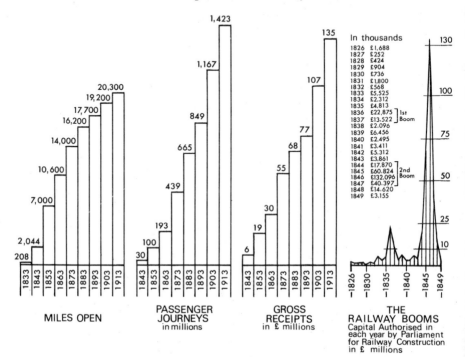

MILES OPEN	PASSENGER JOURNEYS in millions	GROSS RECEIPTS in £ millions	THE RAILWAY BOOMS Capital Authorised in each year by Parliament for Railway Construction in £ millions

In thousands

1826	£1,688	
1827	£252	
1828	£424	
1829	£904	
1830	£736	
1831	£1,800	
1832	£568	
1833	£5,525	
1834	£2,312	
1835	£4,813	
1836	£22,875	1st Boom
1837	£13,522	
1838	£2,096	
1839	£6,456	
1840	£2,495	
1841	£3,411	
1842	£5,312	
1843	£3,861	
1844	£17,870	2nd Boom
1845	£60,824	
1846	£132,096	
1847	£40,397	
1848	£14,620	
1849	£3,155	

MILES OPEN: 208, 2,044, 7,000, 10,600, 14,000, 16,200, 17,700, 19,200, 20,300

PASSENGER JOURNEYS: 30, 100, 193, 439, 665, 849, 1,167, 1,423

GROSS RECEIPTS: 6, 19, 30, 55, 68, 77, 107, 135

3b. British railway development 1833–1913

Comment

Plate 3a shows a pack-horse train. Each horse carried about $\frac{1}{2}$ cwt.; the coal, iron and textile industries used thousands of tons of material each week, so that a transport revolution was essential.

Plate 3b The building of railways required huge sums of money. This money was provided by the investors in the Railway Companies (proving that England was a wealthy country). Companies spent this money and provided employment for thousands of people.

Plate 3c (see page 31) Stephenson had adapted the steam engine in a locomotive, i.e. an iron horse. The railway led to an increased demand for iron, for coal (in the iron works) and for engineering products, and revolutionised travel, as General Dyott noted (Document 9).

Questions

a. More coal, iron and cotton had to be transported because of industrial change (page 33). How does Plate 3a show that a transport revolution was essential?

b. Why would a horse-train (Plate 3a) be unable to carry sufficient material: (i) to build a new town; (ii) to feed a town of 300,000?

c. Compare the load carried by a horse with that which could be carried behind the Rocket. (See Plate 3c.)

d. The histogram shows how much capital was invested in the building of railways (1826–49). Can you name three materials which had to be bought, and three industries which benefited from this investment?

e. How does this plate and the histogram help you to understand:
(i) the importance of railway development in industrial progess;
(ii) the presence in England of skilled engineers and workmen;
(iii) the presence in England of a rich investing class?

9 From Stage-coach to Railway Coach

1813. I found a very good stage-coach that left Bath at eight in the morning and was two days on the road for London.

1825. I went with my sons to Birmingham on their way back to Westminster; they started in the Eclipse coach at eight o'clock and arrived at Islington exactly at half-past eight in the evening. What a strange alteration from when I went to school.

1826. In consequence of the extraordinary advantage arising to the proprietors of shares in many of the canals . . . a scheme has been proposed for making a railway from Liverpool to Birmingham and from the former to London . . . all the projected shares in the new undertaking are disposed of. Great opposition is expected to the measure in Parliament . . . [from] the present proprietors of canal stock, . . .

1827. I should imagine that travelling must have arrived at perfection from the very fine state of the roads and goodness of the horses. We travelled from the Lee, ninety-nine miles, in little more than twelve hours, including a stoppage to dine.

1830. I took a seat at Liverpool in that mail to London. One of our companions from Coventry was a person employed in surveying and taking levels of the line for the proposed railway from Birmingham to London. It will be a work of great magnitude and extent, and if carried into effect will render highways, horses, and canals useless.

1837. I set out on an excursion to Liverpool per the railway . . . We left Birmingham at half-past eleven, and arrived at Liverpool precisely at four, without the smallest inconvenience; the trains stopped for five minutes at the different stations merely to deliver and to take up passengers and parcels. The speed is so great it is scarce possible to gauge of the country you pass. The tunnel into Liverpool is a grand production of human effort. The railways from Manchester and Birmingham must contribute greatly to Liverpool's increasing wealth and commerce.

William Dyott, *Diary 1781–1845*, ed. R. W. Jefferey, 2 vols, 1902.

3c. Stephenson's Rocket. This steam engine won the prize of £500 at the Rainhill competition of October 1829. It can be seen in the Science Museum, London.

Comment

General Dyott, the author of the diary from which this extract is taken, was impressed by the changes that had taken place in road transport by 1827. The roads could not have carried the bulky goods — coal, china clay, iron ore, building material — being used in industrial England, hence the development of canals (see Document 10). The coming of railways with even greater speed was one of the causes of even more rapid industrial expansion.

Questions

a. How long did it take in 1813 to go from Birmingham to London?

b. What evidence is there that road transport had improved by 1825? And by 1827?

c. Did the shareholders in canal companies make large profits? How did this affect investment in railway company shares? (See Plate 3b.)

d. Give two reasons why the railways affected the income of canal owners.

e. How long did it take to go from Birmingham to Liverpool in 1837?

f. How does the document help to explain the fall in prices of goods which resulted from the coming of the railways?

g. How does the document help to explain: (i) the local nature of the market for goods in the 18th century; (ii) the reasons why few people travelled away from their villages?

h. Why did the railway companies have to issue shares? Why did this mean increased employment in: (i) the iron industry; (ii) the coal industry? (See Plate 3b.)

10 Travelling by Canal

We left Manchester on Monday morning and embarked upon the canal in a stage-boat, bound for Chester . . . This was a new mode of travelling, and a delightful one . . . The shape of the machine resembles the common representations of Noah's Ark, except that the roof is flatter, so made for the convenience of passengers. Within this floating house are two apartments, seats in which are hired at different prices, the parlour and the kitchen. Two horses, harnessed one before the other, tow it along at a rate of a league an hour; [a] pace which it is pleasant to keep up with when walking on the bank. The canal is just wide enough for two boats to pass.

England is now intersected in every direction by canals. This is the district in which they were first tried by the present Duke of Bridgewater, whose fortune has been amply increased by the success of his experiment. His engineer, Brindley, was a singular character, a man of real genius for this particular employment, who thought of nothing but locks and levels, perforating hills, and floating barges upon aqueduct bridges over unmanageable streams.

Excellent as these canals are, railroads are found to accomplish the same purpose at less expense. In these, the wheels of the carriage move in grooves upon iron bars laid all along the road; where there is a descent no draught is required, and the laden waggons as they run down draw the empty ones up. These roads are always used in the neighbourhood of coal-mines and foundries. It has been recommended . . . that they should be universally introduced, and a hope held out that at some future time this will be done . . . If this be at present one of the dreams of philosophy, it is a philosophy by which trade and manufactures would be benefited and money saved; and the dream therefore may probably one day be accomplished.

R. Southey, *Espriella's letters from England,* 1807.

Comment

The amount of coal and iron, clay and building material, food and textiles being carried increased. Abraham Darby had invented one method of dealing with this (Document 7); the Duke of Bridgewater financed the building of a canal designed and built by Brindley. Each canal owner (and/or builder) had his own ideas of width and depth, so that there was no uniformity between canals.

The railway companies learned from these mistakes. Most of the companies soon agreed on a common width — so that 'through travel' became possible. They also became 'common carriers' themselves, providing not only the 'way' but the 'means'.

Questions

a. What did the barge look like: (i) from the outside; (ii) inside?
b. How was the barge pulled along?
c. How do you know that there were many canals in England? Who (i) paid for, (ii) designed the first one?
d. How did Brindley and other canal builders take their canals through different ground levels?
e. How did the first railways work?
f. Why were canals not made wider at the beginning? Why did it prove very difficult and costly to widen them later?
g. What lessons did the railway companies learn from the experience of the canal builders? (Think of finance, building and operation.)
h. Write a paragraph on: (i) Brindley; (ii) the problems of canal building.

11 Railways versus Canals

On the introduction of railways, . . . when want of experience . . . rendered it impossible for the [Government] to impose proper restrictions . . . on the . . . charges of the various companies, competition . . . with the canals checked any great abuse of the powers delegated to them, . . . and the . . . competition . . . reduced the expense of conveyance. Instances have been adduced before your Committee in which the charges for the conveyance of merchandize have been lowered by these means to one-seventh of their former amount; and . . . few parts of the country have not derived material advantage from the competition between railways and canals.

Parliament should not lightly sanction any arrangements which would tend to deprive the public of this advantage. . . .

One great impediment has been found to exist in the present disjointed state of the canal interests . . . Some of the existing companies, possessing lines of canal which form central links in a great chain, take advantage of their peculiar position, and establish a [high] rate of charges . . . This practice obliges the other companies . . . to reduce their rates [and] they are unable to conduct their business at a profit. At the same time [it] prevents such a reduction in the general charges of the line as would enable the companies to maintain a fair competition with the Railways.

Railway companies have effected private arrangements with the proprietors of a portion only of a line of canal, and by raising the tolls of that portion to the utmost limit allowed by law, have rendered it impossible for the companies in possession of the remainder of the line of canal to maintain their traffic in competition with the railway.

Second Report of Select Committee on Amalgamation of Railways and Canals, Parliamentary Papers, 1846, XIII.

3d. The rivals: on the right, the tunnel at Foxes Wood, near Bristol, built for the new railway; on the left, the canal.

Comment

This is an extract from a Report by a Parliamentary Committee set up because of the large number of Bills being put forward for the amalgamation of railway and canal companies.

At first there had been competition between the two forms of transport: increasingly the canals were incapable of competing with the new railways — which were quicker and cheaper, and provided 'through' traffic facilities.

Questions

a. What evidence does this document offer that the Government interfered in the operation of railways and canals from an early date?
b. What evidence does the document offer on the cost of transport?
c. How did this affect coal-using factories, textile manufacturers and the housewife?
d. Show, on a sketch, how one canal formed a link in a chain.
e. How did such 'link' canals help the railway companies?
f. Why were most canals unable to compete with railways?
g. What light does the document throw on canal construction and ownership?
h. Write a paragraph on: (i) the Railway Act, 1844; (ii) George Hudson.

12 The Social Benefits of a Railway

Success to the Newport Railway,
Along the braes of the Silvery Tay,
And to Dundee straightway,
Across the Railway Bridge o' the Silvery Tay,
Which was opened on the 12th of May,
In the year of our Lord 1879,
Which will clear all expenses in a very short time;
Because the thrifty housewives of Newport
To Dundee will often resort,
Which will be to them profit and sport,
By bringing cheap tea, bread, and jam,
And also some of Lipton's ham,
Which will make their hearts feel light and gay,
And cause them to bless the opening day
Of the Newport Railway.
The train is most beautiful to be seen,
With its long, white curling cloud of steam,
As the train passes on her way
Along the bonnie braes o' the Silvery Tay.
And if the people of Dundee
Should feel inclined to have a spree,
I am sure 'twill fill their hearts with glee
By crossing o'er to Newport,
And there they can have excellent sport,
By viewing the scenery beautiful and gay,
During the livelong summer day,
And then they can return at night
With spirits light and gay,
By the Newport Railway,
By night or by day,
Across the Railway Bridge o' the Silvery Tay.

William McGonagall, *The Newport Railway.*

Comment

This poem refers to only one railway line, but the ideas in the poem apply equally to all railway lines.

The housewives could buy cheaper food (carried by railway to Dundee) in chain stores (only possible with railways). The fuller standard of living enjoyed by their families helped to provide employment for other people in producing, distributing and selling these goods (Section 6).

The housewives could also buy a wide variety of clothing, and fashions could now be national, not only for London. Women would read about the fashions in their new daily national press, and buy the clothes in national stores. Cheap fares were provided to attract these housewives, whose husbands might travel to work on workmen's trains.

Questions

a. Why would the railway line clear all its expenses?

b. Why were prices lower after the coming of the railway?

c. What 'sport' or 'spree' was possible in the bigger towns but not in the smaller towns?

d. Using Document 9 and the pictures on page 28, show how the life of the people was changed by transport changes.

e. Why were goods only locally produced and sold in 1700 but nationally distributed in 1900?

f. What is the significance of 'Lipton's ham' in the document?

g. What were (i) three social, (ii) three economic effects of railway development?

h. How did this development help in the rise of the national press?

4a. Oldham was one of the chief centres of the cotton-spinning industry

13 Towns, Old and New

Comment

Oldham is typical of the industrial towns. The large number of high chimney stacks indicate the number of factories. Around each were built row after row of small houses. The town just grew — unplanned. Often there was no local council (Document 5); until the 1848 Public Health Act there were no laws to prevent the building of overcrowded and unventilated streets which were often not drained or cleansed. Sometimes a group of enlightened business men obtained an Act of Parliament to try and improve matters (Document 14); there were attempts at town planning by men like Titus Salt.

4b. A recent attempt to make living in towns more pleasant: Cumbernauld, Dumbarton, 1966

Questions

a. There are a number of tall stacks in Plate 4a. How do they illustrate: (i) the number of factories; (ii) the demand for coal in the area of Oldham?
b. There are fewer stacks in Plate 4b. What power is used to drive the machinery in the modern factory?
c. The houses are built near the factories (Plate 4a). Why did workpeople have to live near their place of work in the early 19th century?
d. The houses were built by the factory owner or by a speculative builder. Why did they leave so little space between the houses?
e. Why was Oldham an unhealthy town?

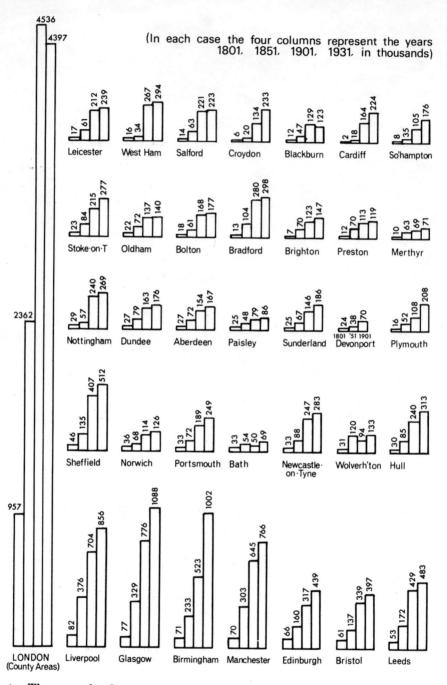

(In each case the four columns represent the years 1801, 1851, 1901, 1931, in thousands)

4c. The growth of towns 1801–1931

Comment

The rapidity of the growth of some towns can be seen. A huge increase in population, demanding homes but earning little (Document 14), was bound to lead to poor housing conditions and a high mortality rate (Section 6).

Some towns grew rapidly and then stopped when they felt the sting of foreign competition (Book II, Section 2). Other towns with a more varied industrial base continued to grow. Other towns had a poor growth rate, because they had no economic facilities. These changes in size are of some significance in explaining the movement for Parliamentary Reform (Documents 41 and 42).

Questions

a. Mark the growing towns on a map.
b. How do these histograms illustrate the movement of population which was a feature of the Industrial Revolution?
c. Which industry developed at Blackburn, Preston and Oldham?
d. Explain the slow rate of growth of these towns after 1900.
e. What industries are centred on Sheffield and Birmingham?
f. Why did these towns continue to grow?
g. If Manchester had no effective local government (Document 14), what was likely to have been the position in Birmingham and Merthyr?
h. Find out the dates of the incorporation of Leeds, Manchester and Birmingham.

14 Manchester, 1840

Until twelve years ago there was no paving and [sewage] Act in the township of Manchester, containing in the year 1831 upwards of 142,000 inhabitants . . . At the present time the paving of the streets proceeds rapidly in every direction, and great attention is given to the drains. It is gratifying to bear testimony to the zeal of the authorities in carrying on the salutary improvements, especially when it is known that no street can be paved and sewered without the consent of the owners of property. Owing to this cause several important streets remain to this hour disgraceful nuisances.

Manchester has no Building Act, and hence, with the exception of certain central streets, over which the Police Act gives the Commissioners power, each proprietor builds as he pleases. New cottages, . . . huddled together row behind row, may be seen springing up in many parts . . . The authorities cannot interfere. A cottage row may be badly drained, the streets may be full of pits, brimful of stagnant water, the receptacle of dead cats and dogs, yet no-one may find fault.

Food is dear, labour scarce, and wages in many branches very low; . . . disease and death are making unusual havoc. It is in such a depressed state of the manufacturing districts as at present exists that unpaved and badly sewered streets exhibit their malign influence on young and old . . .

Manchester has no public park . . . where the population can walk and breathe the fresh air. New streets are rapidly extending in every direction, and those who live in more populous quarters can seldom hope to see the green face of nature.

John Robertson, Surgeon, in *Report of Committee on Health of Towns*, No. XI, 1840.

Comment

Manchester was one of the rapidly growing towns which had not been incorporated (Document 5) even by 1840. The local government was the court leet of the Mosley owner of the manor. Some local leaders, such as doctors and employers, had worked for local Acts of Parliament which set up new governing bodies for specific purposes; but the powers given to these bodies were limited, as this extract makes clear.

Questions

a. When did Manchester obtain a paving and sewerage Act? Name two other Acts mentioned in the extract.

b. Why did 'several important streets remain . . . nuisances'?

c. What attitude on the part of property owners does this extract illustrate?

d. Which Act gave 'the Commissioners power'? What powers were they given?

e. Give an example from the document to show why lack of legislation allowed slums to be built.

f. How would the extract help you to understand the phrase 'the Hungry Forties'?

g. 'Manchester has no public park.' In addition to the park, what amenities does your local government provide today?

h. How does this document help to explain the high death rates in working-class areas? (See also Plate 4a.)

15 Regulation Issued by Board of Health, 1849

To the Guardian of the Poor named in the Schedules hereunto annexed:

Councils and other Governing Bodies, by Law intrusted with the Care and Management of the Streets and Public Ways and Places within the said Unions and Parishes; the Owners and Occupiers of Houses, within the said Unions and Parishes; and to all to whom it may concern.

We, the General Board of Health, are authorized to issue such directions . . . as the . . . Board shall think fit for the prevention of . . . disease; these directions . . . shall extend to all parts or places in which the . . . Act shall . . . be in force . . .

. . . We direct that all . . . bodies . . . intrusted with the care and management of the streets, and public ways and places, . . . shall . . . once in every twenty-four hours . . . cleanse all such of the streets, under their respective care and management, as by the medical officer of the guardians, shall be certified to be in a state dangerous to health.

Where any such streets to which any houses or tenements adjoin, which have not been intrusted by law to the care or management of any council, have been certified . . . to be in a state dangerous to health, we direct that every occupier of a house shall keep or cause to be kept sufficiently cleansed, at least once in every twenty-four hours such parts as adjoins the house or tenement occupied by him, by effectual washing or otherwise, and with the use of such fluids or substances as the medical officer of the guardians shall think necessary . . .

We do hereby authorize and require the guardians to superintend and see to the execution of the foregoing directions and where it shall appear that by want of the council, or by reason of poverty of the occupiers there may be any default in the cleansing of any street, we authorize the guardians to cause such street to be effectually cleansed.

Report of the Board of Health, July 1849.

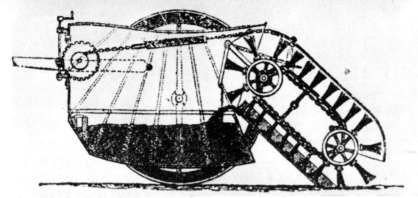

4d. This road-sweeping machine was only one of Joseph Whitworth's many inventions. During the 1840s it is said to have made Manchester one of the cleanest of the large English towns.

Comment

Edwin Chadwick was the mainspring of the new Poor Law system (Section 7). He had, in this, an administrative system, i.e. the local Boards of Guardians and the supervisory Poor Law Commission in London. He had proposed in 1842 (Document 16) that sanitary administration should be made the responsibility of the Guardians, who were already concerned with financing the ill-effects of insanitary conditions (Document 21).

When the Board of Health was set up in 1848, it had to deal with a multiplicity of local authorities which refused to give up their powers to one single authority. Also, the Board had no effective way of enforcing its regulations.

Questions

a. List the four different bodies responsible for the care of the streets.
b. What authority did the General Board have?
c. Who was supposed to clean the streets?
d. What part was to be played by the medical officer of the Guardians?
e. Who was supposed to see that the Board's directions were carried out?
f. When should Guardians see to cleansing of streets?
g. Write a paragraph on Edwin Chadwick.
h. Explain why (i) some property owners, (ii) some ratepayers, (iii) some authorities opposed Chadwick.

16 Early Examples
of 'Socialism', 1842

... In Manchester gas has for some years been supplied from works erected and conducted by a body appointed (under a local Act) by an elected committee of the ratepayers ... and the supplies of gas are of a better quality, and cheaper than those obtained from private companies in adjacent towns; improvements ... are more speedily adopted than in private associations, and the profits are reserved as a public fund ... Out of this fund a fine Town Hall has been erected, streets widened, and various large improvements made. The income now available for the further improvement of the town exceeds £10,000 per annum ... There are now in the same districts in [London] no less than three immense capitals sunk in competition, — three sets of gas-pipes [in] the same streets, three ... sets of ... offices where one would suffice, comparatively high charges for gas to the consumers, and low dividends to the shareholders of the companies ... A proposal was made in Manchester to obtain supplies of water for the town in the same manner as the supplies of gas, but the owners of the private pumps, who have the monopoly of the convenient springs, and exact double the charge for which even private companies are ready to convey supplies into the houses, made ... effectual opposition to the proposal, contending that the supplies of rain-water (which are sometimes absolutely black with the soot held in suspension), together with that from the springs was sufficient, and the proposal was defeated. ...

There appears to be no reason to doubt that the mode of supplying gas to the town of Manchester might be generally adopted in supplying water to the population.

Chadwick, *Report on the Sanitary Conditions of the Labouring Population*, 1842.

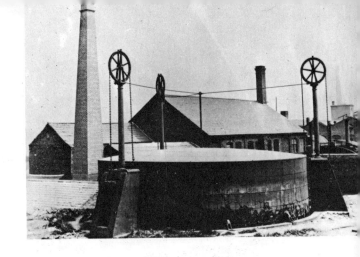

4e. Murdock's original gas-holder. It was first used for coal gas in 1798.

Comment

This extract is taken from a Report on the sanitary conditions of the Labouring Population by Chadwick in 1842. Again we have an example of a local Act obtained for a specific purpose, to permit a municipal gas company to be formed in Manchester. The advantages for Manchester are listed and compared with the disadvantages of the private supply system in London.

Chadwick was a believer in freedom (Document 36), but work with the Poor Law Commission showed him that a strong local government with reasonable powers was required to improve sanitary conditions. He said that a municipal authority alone could provide the amenity on the scale and at the price which people required and could afford (Plate 9).

Questions

a. What were the advantages of a municipal gas supply: (i) to the customer; (ii) for production?

b. How had Manchester benefited?

c. What groups might oppose an extension of this system to other towns?

d. Why did Manchester not have a municipal water supply?

e. What two sources of water were available to people of Manchester?

f. How does the evidence in this document help to explain high death-rates (Document 21)?

g. Use Documents 14, 15 and 16 to show that attempts were made to deal with the problem of town development.

5a. Children being lowered into coal-mine, about 1840

5b. Two children struggling to carry the coal to the surface

5c. A boy dragging a coal-sledge to the shaft

5d. ·A nineteenth-century representation of a mining explosion. These explosions were usually caused by methane, a gas which came out of the coal, and accumulated in the crevices. The gas was ignited by a spark. The invention of Davy's safety lamp in 1815 made this risk less.

Comment

The first Factory Acts dealt with the textile factories (Document 19), and young children could not be employed. It was not until 1840 that conditions in the coal-mines became widely known, an increased demand for coal (Documents 6, 7 and 11 and Plate 3c) led to increased employment in coal-mining areas. Mine owners found that some of the work could best be done by children.

The coal was cut by a miner and loaded on to a small sledge (Plate 5c). This was then pulled by a boy or girl from the coal face to the point where it was taken to the surface (Plate 5c).

Questions

a. How could the child see where he was going?
b. What is the child pulling?
c. Why does he not stand upright?
d. Why were accidents likely when the coal was being taken to the surface (Plate 5b)?
e. Reports often spoke of the brutal nature of people in mining areas. Why would you expect brutal behaviour from people working in these conditions?

17 Self-help — The Road to Success

The greatest results in life are usually attained by simple means and . . . ordinary qualities. The common life of every day, with its cares, necessities, and duties, affords . . . opportunity for acquiring experience of the best kind; and its most beaten paths provide the worker with scope for effort and self-improvement. The high-road of human welfare lies along the highway of steadfast well-doing; and they who are the most persistent . . . will be the most successful.

There is a famous speech recorded of a Norseman, thoroughly characteristic of the Teuton. 'I believe neither in idols nor demons,' said he, 'I put my sole trust in my own strength of body and soul.' The ancient crest on a pickaxe with the motto of 'Either I will find a way or make one', was an expression of the same independence and practical materialism, which to this day distinguishes the descendants of the Northmen.

Energy enables a man to force his way through irksome drudgery . . . and carries him onward and upward in every station in life. It accomplishes more than genius . . . It is not eminent talent that is required to ensure success in any pursuit, so much as purpose — not merely the power to achieve, but the will to labour . . . perseveringly. Even if a man fails in his efforts, it will be a great satisfaction to him to enjoy the consciousness of having done his best. In humble life nothing can be more cheering and beautiful than to see a man combating suffering by patience . . . and who, when his feet are bleeding and his limbs failing him, still walks upon his courage.

Samuel Smiles, *Self-Help*, 1859.

Comment

Samuel Smiles was the author of a number of books which encouraged the belief that to achieve success was a simple matter.

Even Smiles was forced to admit the possibility of failure. Failure, however, merely called for more virtues, such as resignation, patience and fortitude.

Questions

a. How, according to Smiles, would people achieve the greatest results?
b. Why does the evidence of Document 14 suggest that the road to self-improvement was not as simple as Smiles believed?
c. Why could the old Norseman make his own way without aid?
d. What was required to ensure success? What might a child worker (Plate 5) have said about this?
e. What did Smiles consider 'beautiful'?
f. Why might the people of Manchester (Document 14) have argued that this was not beautiful?
g. How would Smiles' ideas have been used in the debates on Factory Acts, Housing Acts and Poor Law Reform?
h. In what ways has the State aided your improvement?

18 The Argument Against Factory Acts

Under the present law, no mill in which persons under eighteen years of age are employed (and, therefore, scarcely any mill at all) can be worked more than eleven and a half hours a day, that is, twelve hours for five days in the week and nine on Saturday.

Now, the following analysis will show that, in a mill so worked, the whole net profit is derived *from the last hour*. I will suppose a manufacturer to invest £100,000; £80,000 in his mill and machinery, and £20,000 in raw materials and wages. The annual return of that mill, supposing . . . gross profits to be fifteen per cent., ought to be goods worth £115,000 . . . Of this £115,000, each of the twenty-three half hours of work produces one twenty-third. . . . £100,000 out of the £115,000 makes up for the deterioration of the mill and machinery. The remaining 2-23rds., that is the last two of the twenty-three half hours of every day, produce the net profit of ten per cent. If, therefore, (prices remaining the same) the factory could be kept at work thirteen hours instead of eleven and a half, . . . the net profit would be more than doubled. On the other hand, if the hours of working were reduced by one hour per day (prices remaining the same), net profit would be destroyed — if they were reduced by an hour and a half, even *gross* profit would be destroyed. . . . there would be no fund to compensate the progressive deterioration of the fixed capital . . .

Nassau W. Senior, *Letters on the Factory Act*, 1837.

Comment

This extract is from a letter written in 1837 when Parliament was debating a ten-hour Bill (which was rejected). The writer, Nassau Senior, was an economist; along with Adam Smith, Ricardo and Malthus, he might be said to have started the subject of economics. He took an active part in national affairs, as a member of a number of Commissions, and notably the Poor Law Commission (1834).

He was writing to the President of the Board of Trade. Elsewhere in the letter he asserts that work in the cotton factories was light and easy, that shortening the working day would lead to increased prices, a fall in the demand for cotton goods and ruin for the British cotton industry.

Questions

a. State the 'law' referred to in the opening line.
b. To which industry did that 'law' apply? Why did Senior talk about a 'mill' and not a 'factory'?
c. Why was his argument called 'the last hour'?
d. How much did the mill cost: (i) to set up; (ii) to run?
e. What was the gross annual profit?
f. What were the goods produced worth?
g. What alternative hours of work were suggested?
h. Why did (i) Smiles, (ii) Senior hold out little hope for the working class?

19 The Factory Act of 1833

. . . no person under eighteen years of age shall [work] between half-past eight in the evening and half-past five in the morning, in any cotton, woollen, worsted, hemp, flax, tow, linen, or silk mill . . .

. . . no person under the age of eighteen shall be employed in any such mill . . . more than twelve hours in . . . one day, nor more than sixty-nine hours in . . . one week.

There shall be allowed . . . not less than one and a half hours for meals.

It shall not be lawful . . . to employ in any factory . . . as aforesaid, except in mills for the manufacture of silk, any child who shall not have completed his or her ninth year.

It shall not be lawful for any person to employ . . . in any factory . . . as aforesaid for longer than forty-eight hours in one week, nor for longer than nine hours in one day, any child who shall not have completed his or her eleventh year . . .

It shall be lawful for His Majesty to appoint four Inspectors of factories where . . . children and young persons under eighteen years of age [are] employed, empowered to enter any . . . mill, and any school . . . belonging thereto, at all times . . . by day or by night, when such . . . factories are at work.

The Inspectors shall have power to make such rules as may be necessary for the execution of this act, binding on all persons subject to the provisions of this act; and are authorised to enforce the attendance at school of children employed in factories according to the provisions of this act.

Every child restricted to the performance of forty-eight hours of labour in any one week shall attend some school.

Statutes of the Realm, 3 & 4 William IV, c. 103.

Comment

These extracts are from the first effective Factory Act, passed in 1833 by a Whig Government. The document illustrates both the strong and weak points of the Act, and gives an idea of what conditions had been in textile mills, and remained in most other industries.

The great strength of the Act lay in the appointment of four Inspectors by the Crown. This was obviously a ridiculously small number, but a crucial first step had been taken in the right direction (see Document 36).

Questions

a. To what factories did the Act apply?
b. What did the Act say about persons under eighteen?
c. What did the Act say about persons: (i) under eleven; (ii) under nine?
d. How many Inspectors were appointed? What were they to do?
e. What was said about meals and schools?
f. Why was the Act relating to the Registration of Births, Marriages and Deaths so important with regard to Factory Acts?
g. What does the Act say about the silk industry? In which other industry (Plate 5) did young children work?
h. Give the date for the principal Factory Act which led to the ten-hour day.

20 A Progressive Factory Owner

... As to the conclusions I have come to from the working of my ... mill, ... for 11 instead of 12 hours each day, as previously, I am quite satisfied that both as much yarn and ... cloth may be produced at quite as low a cost in 11 as in 12 hours ...; it is my ... intention to make a further reduction to $10\frac{1}{2}$ hours, without the slightest fear of suffering loss ... I find the hands work with greater energy and spirit; they are more cheerful, and ... happy. All the arguments I have heard in favour of long time appear based on an arithmetical question — if 11 produce so much, what will 12 or 15 hours produce? This is correct, [for] the steam-engine, but try this on the horse, and you will ... find he cannot compete with the engine, as he requires time to rest and feed.

There is more bad work made the last one or two hours of the day than the whole of the first nine or ten hours.

... About 20 years ago, we had many orders for a style of goods ... We had about 30 young women ... in our Manchester warehouse; ... I requested that they would work (instead of 11) 12 hours. At the end of the week, I found they had not a mere trifle more work done; but, supposing there was some incidental cause for this, I requested they would work 13 hours the following week, at the end of which they had produced less instead of more work. The overlooker ... invited me to be in the room with them the last hour of the day. They were exhausted and making bad work and little of it; I therefore reduced their time two hours, as before. Since that time I have been an advocate for shorter hours of labour.

Parliamentary Papers, 1845, xxv, pp. 456–7.

Comment

This is an extract from a letter written by a Lancashire factory owner to the chairman of a meeting being held to discuss the demand for a shorter working week. From 1833 to 1847 humanitarians, enlightened

5e. The factory of Swainson, Bailey and Company near Preston, Lancashire, shows that some owners tried to provide good conditions for their workers

factory owners, radical politicians and working-class leaders were advocating a ten-hour day. The opposition to this was led by the economists (Document 18), who were reflecting the belief which Smiles had advocated (Document 17).

There were many 'good' factory owners and most of the large mills were well run. It was the smaller workshop, often in a garret, which provided the worst examples of bad conditions, and regulation was essential to improve these.

Questions

a. What did Gardner (the Lancashire factory owner) say about the cost of yarn produced in 11 hours?
b. What did he say about the quality of that yarn?
c. What working day did he intend to bring in?
d. How did the shorter day affect the workers?
e. What had he to say about the work produced in the last hour?
f. Why is it not possible for people to work like machines?
g. How does Gardner's experience of the last hour compare with Senior's theory (Document 18)?
h. Write a paragraph on the work of Lord Shaftesbury. Show that many factory owners would support his work.

Comment

England was a wealthy country as the figures on page 40 indicated. Among the owners of the wealth were the middle class, . . . who lived in the larger houses built on the outskirts of the industrial towns and in the more select areas of London.

Plate 6a shows a kitchen from such a house.

The lady of the house would have to supervise the servants: for this she would require Mrs. Beeton's 'Book of Household Management'. This 1,172-paged book priced 7s. 6d. sold over 2 million copies between 1861 and 1870, another indication of the affluence of middle-class society.

Questions

a. How many people are there in Plate 6a?
b. Look at the number of saucepans, jugs and the utensils. How does this show that servants were necessary?
c. What was the method of cooking (Plate 6b)? How did this make the work of housekeeping harder for the Victorians than for modern women?
d. Look again at Plate 4a. Why was it unlikely that this kitchen (Plate 6a) belonged to the houses in the foreground of Plate 4a?
e. How does the kitchen (Plate 6a) help you to understand Victorian affluence?

6a. A prosperous middle-class Victorian kitchen, about 1889

6b. The kitchen of a rather less well-off Victorian family. The open fire has been converted to make room for the oven.

21 The Effects of Unsanitary Conditions on Different Classes

Mr. Wood was asked:
'You have seen the following returns of the average ages of death amongst the different classes of people in Manchester and Rutland

Average age of death	In Manchester	In Rutland(shire)
Professional persons and gentry and families	38	52
Tradesmen and their families	20	41
Mechanics, labourers and families	17	38

'. . . Are the different chances of life amongst each class of the population . . . conformable to what you would have anticipated from your examinations of the houses, and . . . of the inhabitants?'

'They are. . . . That opinion is erroneous which ascribes greater . . . mortality to the children employed in factories than [to] children who remain in such homes as these towns afford to the labouring classes. Of all who are born of the labouring classes in Manchester, more than 57% die before they attain 5 years of age; that is before they can be engaged in factory labour. At the period between 5 and 10 years of age the proportion of deaths which occur amongst the labouring classes . . . [is] not so great as the proportion of deaths which occur amongst the children of the middle classes who are not so engaged; . . . [thus] the effect of employment is not shown to be injurious in any increase of the proportion who die . . .

'But in Liverpool (which is a commercial and not a manufacturing town) where the condition of the dwellings are reported to be the worst — there the chances of life . . . [are] still lower than in Manchester, [or] Leeds. (In Liverpool), of the deaths which occurred amongst the labouring classes, . . . 62% . . . [were] under 5 years of age. For Birmingham, where there are many insalubrious manufactories but where the drainage is comparatively good, the proportion of mortality was, in 1838, 1 in 40; whilst in Liverpool it was 1 in 31.'

Evidence presented in Chadwick's *Report on the Sanitary Conditions of the Labouring Population*, 1842.

Comment

Chadwick had been appointed to yet another Royal Commission, one to enquire into the Sanitary Conditions of the Labouring Classes. This meant an examination of the housing conditions of the new industrial towns; and we know, from the documents in Section 4, what he found there (see Plate 4a). What he also found was that a person's chances of remaining alive depended on the class into which he was born, and the sort of district in which he was born. This is clear from the figures in paragraph 1.

These deaths were 'preventible' because they could be prevented under right conditions. It has been the aim of the Government in the past 100 years to create a social system which has reduced 'preventible' deaths.

Questions

a. What was the expectation of life for the different classes in Manchester?

b. How did this compare with the expectation of life in Rutlandshire?

c. Can you suggest three reasons why the labourer in Rutlandshire had as high an expectation of life as the gentry in Manchester?

d. What connection did Mr. Wood find between housing conditions and the expectation of life: (i) in Manchester; (ii) in Liverpool?

e. What percentage of labourers' children died before the age of 5: (i) in Manchester; (ii) in Liverpool? At what age did they begin work in factories?

f. How did Mr. Wood show that factory work was not injurious to health?

g. Compare the infant mortality rate for Birmingham with that for Liverpool. What, according to Mr. Wood, was the main cause of the difference?

h. Why did findings like these call for increased state activity, as outlined in Documents 35 and 36?

22 Working-class Life in 1832

The population employed in the cotton factories rises at five o'clock, works . . . from six till eight o'clock, and returns home for half an hour . . . to breakfast. This meal generally consists of tea or coffee with a little bread. Oatmeal porridge is sometimes, but, of late, rarely used . . . The tea is almost always of a bad quality; little or no milk is added. The operatives return to the mills until twelve o'clock when an hour is allowed for dinner. Amongst those who obtain the lower rate of wages this meal generally consists of boiled potatoes. The mess of potatoes is put into one large dish and a few pieces of fried fat bacon are sometimes mingled with them, but seldom meat. Those who obtain better wages, or families whose total income is larger, add a greater proportion of meat to this meal, at least three times a week; but the quantity consumed by the labouring classes is not great. The family sits round the table and they all plunge their spoons into the dish with an animal eagerness . . . At the end of the hour they are all again employed in the mills, where they continue until seven o'clock or a later hour, when they generally again indulge in tea, often mingled with spirits accompanied by a little bread.

The wages obtained by operatives are, in general, sufficient to provide them with the decent comforts of life; the average wages of all persons employed in the mills (young and old) being from nine to twelve shillings per week. But the wages of certain classes are exceedingly meagre. . . . More than one-half of the inhabitants . . . require the assistance of public charity.

J. Kay, from *Social Conditions and Education of the People in England and Europe*, 2 vols, 1850.

Comment

The rise of the cotton industry (Document 5) was the cause of the growth of a new industrial area in Lancashire (Document 39) and the growth of large towns (Document 13), such as Manchester (Document 14). Industrial development brought greatly increased wealth for some (Document 24) and ultimately led to higher standards of living for the population as a whole (Document 23). However, the living and working conditions of the workers were improved very slowly. These improvements were brought about by the work of men such as Kay (the author of this extract), progressive factory owners such as Gardner (Document 20) and Owen, and humanitarians like Lord Shaftesbury.

Questions

a. How many hours did the operatives work?

b. What was their average wage: (i) per week; (ii) per hour?

c. How does this document help us to understand: (i) the low rents which most families could afford; (ii) overcrowding?

d. What was their diet?

e. How often did some 'better-off' families have meat?

f. How many people in Manchester were forced to 'require the assistance of' public charity? Why did such people not save for a 'rainy day'?

g. How does this help us to understand the figures given in Document 21?

h. What would Samuel Smiles (Document 17) have said to the complaints of these people?

23 Rising Standards of Living for the Working Classes

... The working classes of the United Kingdom have enjoyed a great improvement in wages in the last fifty years, an improvement roughly estimated at 50 to 100 per cent; the hours of labour have been shortened in the same period 20 per cent; there has been a ... fall in the prices of the principal articles of general consumption, with the exception of rent and meat, where the increase still left to the labourer a large margin for increased ... expenditure; ... the condition of the masses has in fact improved vastly, as is shown by the diminished rate of mortality, the increased consumption per head of tea, sugar, and the like articles, the extension of popular education, the diminution of crime and pauperism, and the increase of savings bank deposits, as well as of other forms of saving among the masses.

Of a non-agricultural kind in [London] and the leading manufacturing towns, the rise [in wages] ranges from 15s. to 25s. or about 70 per cent, but ... there are cases of an advance of 100 per cent.

The ... conclusion ... is, that what has happened to the working classes ... is a revolution ..., having substituted for millions of people ... who were constantly on the brink of starvation, and who suffered untold privations, new millions of artisans and fairly well-paid labourers.

Robert Giffen, *Essays in Finance*, 1887.

Comment

This document was written at the time of the first Jubilee of Queen Victoria (1887) when optimism was high.

The author shows that the standard of living had risen. The national income (i.e. the total of all wealth produced in the country in a year) rose from £232 million in 1801 to £1,642 million in 1901. Part of this increased wealth was used for investment (Document 14). Part also went in increased wages to the working classes, part in social investment (in schools, roads, hospitals, etc.).

6c. A middle-class Victorian family at tea

Questions

a. The average wage in Manchester in the 1830s was 9s. to 12s. (Document 22). What, according to Giffen, was the average wage in the 1880s?

b. What effects had Factory Acts on the length of the working day?

c. If wages go up by 50–100% and prices fall, what effect will this have on the standard of living?

d. Name two articles bought by the working classes in 1887 to indicate a rising standard of living.

e. Why does the growth of savings bank deposits indicate a rising standard of living?

f. Which section of the working classes was, in 1887, still unable to save?

g. Show that the development of railways (Documents 26 and 27) and the coming of Free Trade (Document 40) helped to bring these improvements.

h. How does this document show that Malthus was wrong, at least in the short term?

24 Improved Standards for Middle Classes

Industrialism . . . transformed the home environment of the middle-class family. Gas gave new light to the family parlour . . ., new subscribers to the circulating libraries and, . . ., new cooking stoves to the kitchen. Railways, the agents of suburban colonisation, carried boys to the new public schools and their families to the seaside . . . These, and many other, additions to the physical environment . . . of the middle-class family between the mid-eighteenth and mid-nineteenth centuries are . . . illustrated in the pages of Mrs. Isabella Beeton's 'Book of Household Management'. It was a manual for the middle-class domestic manager, comprising,

> information for the mistress, housekeeper, cook, kitchen-maid, butler, footman, coachman, valet, upper and under house-maids, lady's maid, maid-of-all-work, laundry maid, nurse and nurse-maid, monthly, wet, and sick nurses, etc., etc., also sanitary, medical and legal memoranda: with a history of the origin, properties, and uses, of all things connected with home life and comfort.

The usefulness and appeal of this . . . book . . . can be measured by its sales. . . . It came out as an 1172-page book, price 7s. 6d. in 1861; by 1870 it had sold over two million copies.

The character of the mid-Victorian families . . . had been moulded by many social and economic influences. The middle ranks of society were growing in numbers and in wealth . . . Stable or expanding incomes gave them a settled and optimistic outlook on their economic future.

In 1851 there were more than a million domestic servants, more than double the women and girls then employed in all the textile trades. . . . The household duties of the middle-class wife were limited to supervising, and complaining about, her servants.

O. R. McGregor, *Divorce in England*, 1957.

Comment

We use the term 'the affluent society' to describe Britain in the 1950s and 60s. As this extract shows, the Victorians used very much the same phrase to describe their society; and, of course, in comparison with the past, their generation had 'never had it so good'. This wealth was shared with the working classes (Document 23), but the bulk of the increase went to the middle classes. These were the industrialists, financiers, shopkeepers and professional classes and the employees of local and national government. It was these people and their families who created the demand for education and large houses in suburbia. (See Plate 6.)

6d. This solid building in Bath was typical of many put up in the first half of the nineteenth century

Questions

a. Give three ways in which gas helped to make life easier.
b. Give three ways in which railways affected the middle classes.
c. What was the title of Mrs. Beeton's book? What was its cost? How many copies had been sold in ten years?
d. 'The middle ranks of society were growing in numbers and wealth.' How is this proved?
e. Why were the middle classes optimistic?
f. How many domestic servants were there in 1851? What were the main duties of the middle-class housewife?
g. Arrange the servants mentioned in a better order, to show what part each took in the household.
h. Prices were falling (Document 23). How did this help the middle classes: (i) to enjoy holidays; (ii) to send their children away to school; (iii) save and invest more money?

Comment

Many working people in Bethnal Green lived 'on the verge of pauperism' because: (i) their wages were low; (ii) they were casual labourers, e.g. dockers, dependent on a tide for a job; (iii) they had large families but their wages took no account of this.

These were 'the industrious poor', who had none of the financial advantages of the skilled worker (Document 32). Unable to save, they had no trade union welfare benefits, nor any insurance policies. Unemployment was the result of 'a commercial crisis', and not the fault of the workers; they were driven to the Poor Law authorities and joined the 'hopeless ranks of chronic pauperism'.

A group of philanthropists had provided more than £200 a week to provide employment for some of the workers. This plate shows these men at work. Document 27 refers to a similar experiment at Nottingham. Plate 7b shows another way in which some parents tried to get money — they hired out their children to employers.

Questions

a. What was the cause of unemployment in Bethnal Green in 1866?
b. Why could the workers of Bethnal Green not afford to: (i) save while working; (ii) take out an unemployment policy?
c. What were the aims of the Bethnal Green Employment Association?
d. What work are the men engaged on?
e. Where might the customer in the wine-shop in Plate 7b have got her money?

7a. The labour yard at Bethnal Green, 1868. Efforts were made here to provide work, not just alms, for the poor.

7b. The market for children at Spitalfields, London, 1850. It was the custom to parade all the able-bodied girls, some younger than ten years old, so that employers could select maids.

25 The Speenhamland System Begins, 1795

At a General Meeting of the Justices of this County . . . on Wednesday, the 6th of May, 1795, at the Pelican Inn in Speenhamland . . . for the purpose of rating . . . Wages, Resolved unanimously,

That the present state of the Poor does require further assistance than has been generally given them.

Resolved, That it is not expedient for the Magistrates to grant that assistance by regulating the wages of day labourers, according to the directions of the Statutes of the 5th Elizabeth and 1st James: But the Magistrates very earnestly recommend to the farmers and others throughout the county, to increase the pay of their labourers in proportion to the present price of provisions; and . . . the Magistrates now present have unanimously resolved that they will . . . make the following calculations and allowances for relief of all . . . industrious men and their families who, to the satisfaction of the Justices of their Parish, shall endeavour (as far as they can) for their own support and maintenance.

That is to say, When the loaf of flour, weighing 8 lb. 11 oz. shall cost 1s.

Then every poor and industrious man shall have for his own support 3s. weekly, either produced by his own or his family's labour, or an allowance from the poor rates; and for the support of his wife and every other of his family, 1s. 6d.

When the loaf shall cost 1s. 4d.

Then every poor and industrious man shall have 4s. weekly for his own, and 1s. 10d. for the support of every other of his family.

And . . . as the price of bread rises or falls . . . 3d. to the man, and 1d. to every other of the family, on every 1d. which the loaf rise above 1s.

By order of the Meeting,

W. Budd, Deputy Clerk of the Peace.

Reading Mercury, 11th May 1795.

Comment

The structure of the Poor Law system before 1834 was that set up in the Tudor period. This had the parish as the basis of relief, with local J.P.s supervising unpaid Overseers of the Poor chosen in and by the Parish.

The spread of enclosures after 1750 (Document 2) and the rise in food prices during the French Wars (1793–1815) combined with the decline in cottage industry (Documents 5 and 8) to make life harder for the poor. The magistrates at Speenhamland, near Newbury, Berkshire, organised a system of relief which was copied in many other parishes.

Questions

a. What powers had J.P.s over wages?
b. Why were the poor in need of further assistance in 1795?
c. What has the extract to say about employers and wages?
d. For whom did the Speenhamland magistrates decide to do something?
e. Show how a workman with four children would be affected.
f. Why did this system tempt employers to pay low wages?
g. Why did this lead to an increase in the amount of Poor Rates?
h. Can you see any wage dangers in the new arrangements?

26 The New Poor Law, 1834

The most pressing of the evils . . . are those connected with the relief of the able-bodied. . . . Circumstances will occur in which an individual, by the failure of his means of subsistence, will be exposed to the danger of perishing. To refuse relief is repugnant . . .; therefore, the occurrence of extreme necessity is prevented by almsgiving; [and] the public is warranted in imposing . . . conditions on the individual relieved . . . to the benefit either of the individual himself, or of the country at large . . .

The first . . . of all conditions . . . is that his situation . . . shall not be made . . . as eligible as the situation of the independent labourer of the lowest class. [When] the condition of any pauper class is elevated above the condition of independent labourers, the condition of the independent class is depressed, their industry is impaired, their employment becomes unsteady, and its wages diminished. Such persons, therefore, are under the strongest inducements to quit the less eligible class of labourers, and enter the more eligible class of paupers.

. . . We recommend . . .

First, that except as to medical attendance, . . . all relief to able-bodied persons or families, otherwise than in well-regulated workhouses, shall be declared unlawful, and shall cease.

We recommend . . . the appointment of a Central Board to control the administration of the Poor Laws, with such Assistant Commissioners as may be found requisite; and that the Commissioners be empowered . . . to . . . enforce regulations for the government of workhouses, and the nature and amount of the relief to be given, and the labour to be exacted in them, and that such regulations shall . . . be uniform throughout the country . . .

Report from H.M. Commissioners for enquiring into the Administration . . . of the Poor Laws, 1834.

Comment

The Poor Law Commission was set up by the Whigs who had passed the Reform Bill in 1832, and now had the support of the newly enfranchised industrial middle classes (see Document 34). These resented the continual rise in the poor rates, and believed, like Smiles (Document 17), that poverty and unemployment resulted from defects of character.

The centralised control which the Commission proposed, and which the Act (1834) established, was the first modern administrative machine of the century. Later it was to be used as a model for the Local Government Board, Board of Education, Ministry of Health, etc. (see Document 36).

Questions

a. What is meant by 'able-bodied'? When might an able-bodied man be in 'danger of perishing'?

b. Why was the public justified in imposing conditions?

c. What was the 'standard of eligibility'?

d. Why was this standard applied?

e. Where were the able-bodied to look henceforth for relief?

f. Previously the Poor Law had been administered by local magistrates. Why did the Act of 1834 set up a central supervisory authority?

g. What evidence is there that the Commission wanted to impose a uniform system throughout the whole country?

h. If the pauper was treated as less eligible, what would he do?

27 Nottingham Guardians Forced to Give Outdoor Relief

... The administration of relief by the Board of Guardians had hardly been undertaken before the interruption of the American trade produced a cessation in the demand for labour ... Your Lordship is aware that an opinion has prevailed ... that the provisions of the Poor Law Amendment Act, though useful in the agricultural districts of the south ... of England, are ... inapplicable in ... manufacturing districts ...

We knew that the Union was very inadequately provided with workhouse accommodation. It [had one] old workhouse for about 520 persons ... As the applications for relief increased, ... the Guardians took steps to increase the workhouse accommodation by occupying certain premises belonging to the parish as nurseries for children and as houses for old men, and finally by using a workhouse belonging to the parish of St. Nicholas as a hospital for the sick. They were by these means enabled to provide room for nearly 700 persons ...

... Communication was kept up with the Board of Guardians, from whom we received a weekly report, as well as with our Assistant Commissioner; and it soon became evident that a necessity would speedily arise for relieving more persons than could be provided for within the walls of the workhouses, and ... we felt it to be our duty to authorize ... the Guardians that the rule which prohibited them from giving relief to able-bodied male persons except in the workhouse should be suspended whenever they should find the pressure [created] a necessity for so doing. Preparation was thus made for placing the Guardians in a situation to meet the whole difficulty ... of affording the necessary relief to such destitute persons as might be unable to maintain themselves when thrown out of work.

Third Annual Report of the Poor Law Commission, 1837, Parliamentary Papers, 1837, xxxi.

7c. Dinner-time in
    St.   Pancras
    Workhouse,
    London, 1900

Comment

The Poor Law Commission organised the greater part of the country into Unions of parishes, controlled by Boards of Guardians elected by ratepayers.

In Nottingham, 1836–7, there was general unemployment for the reasons suggested in the extract. The Guardians' workhouse could not cope with a high level of unemployment, and so the Guardians were compelled to give outdoor relief, with the approval of the Poor Law Commission. The workhouse system could not cope with the problems of a wholly industrialised society (see Plate 7).

Questions

a. Why was a decline in trade with America likely to lead to unemployment?
b. Why was the Poor Law Amendment Act, 1834, more suitable for the South than for the North?
c. What was 'a Union'? How many poor could be accommodated in the Nottingham workhouse?
d. Why did this prove insufficient in 1836–7?
e. For what reasons did the Guardians finally give outdoor relief?
f. Which part of the Poor Law Act had the Guardians to suspend?
g. In what ways did the 1834 Act treat the workman as if he was to blame for being unemployed? Why was this obviously not fair in Nottingham in 1836?
h. Why did industrial progress (Document 5, opening lines) lead to increased dangers of unemployment for some?

28 Thomas Carlyle on the New Poor Law, 1839

. . . Why [does] Parliament throw no light on this question of the working classes . . .? . . . It seems surprising, especially in reformed times, to see what space this question occupies in debate . . . Can any other business be so pressing . . .? A reformed Parliament, one would think, should inquire into popular discontents before they get the length of pikes and torches! Yet read Hansard's Debates! . . . All manner of questions and subjects, except this.

The New Poor-Law is an announcement . . . that whosoever will not work ought not to live. Can the poor man that is willing to work always find work, and live by his work? A man willing [but] unable to find work is . . . the saddest sight . . . under the sun.

There is not a horse willing to work but can get food and shelter . . ., a thing the worker has to seek for, to solicit occasionally in vain. . . .

Half a million handloom weavers, working fifteen hours a day, [unable] to procure thereby enough of the coarsest food; English farm-labourers at nine shillings . . . a week; Scotch farm-labourers who '. . . taste no milk, can procure no milk': all these things are credible to us.

. . . The master of horses when the summer . . . is done has to feed his horses through the winter. If he said to his horses: 'Quadrupeds, I have no longer work for you; but work exists abundantly over the world; go and seek [it] . . .' . . . They gallop along highways . . .; finally, under pains of hunger, they take to leaping fences; eating foreign property, and — we know the rest. . . .

Thomas Carlyle, *Treatise on Chartism*, 1839.

Comment

This is an extract from a treatise by Thomas Carlyle in which he said: 'Not that Chartism now exists should provoke wonder, but that the invited hungry people should have sat eight years . . . patiently expecting somewhat from the name of a Reform Ministry, and not till after eight years have grown hopeless. This is the respectable side of the miracle.'

Chartism was a movement for political reform. It was born out of the Poor Law in the hope of achieving social, economic and industrial reform through a reformed Parliament. That this was the fear of the Whigs (Documents 42 and 43) may explain their reluctance to accept the Chartist demands. Improvements did follow the extension of the franchise.

Questions

a. What does he mean by 'reformed times'?

b. What class gained the vote in 1832? What interest did they show in the 'question' of the working classes?

c. Name five Acts passed between 1833 and 1841.

d. Carlyle asked a question in paragraph 2. What was the answer to the question?

e. What evidence is there from this document that the country went through a depression in the late 1830s? (See also Documents 14 and 22.)

f. How does Carlyle show that revolution might occur if conditions did not improve?

g. How does this document foretell the rise of the Chartist movement? (See Plates 8a, 8b and 10b.)

h. What were the main points of the Charter?

Comment

Trade unions could legally be formed after 1824 when the Combination Acts (Document 29) were repealed. The attitude of most of the middle and upper classes was that unions were dangerous and unwanted.

This hostile attitude was shown at the trial of the six men who had formed the Friendly Society of Agricultural Labourers at Tolpuddle in Dorset in October 1833. The local magistrates arrested George Loveless (the leader) and five others, found them guilty of administering unlawful oaths to trade unionists and sentenced them to transportation to Australia.

The Whig Government with Lord Melbourne as Home Secretary supported their decision. They employed spies and encouraged legal action against unions. Plate 8a shows the demonstration against the verdict. Plate 8b shows that even the agricultural worker, unskilled, scattered and poorly paid, had a union in 1871.

Questions

a. Dorchester labourers were sentenced in 1834. Why did they call themselves the 'Victims of Whiggery'?
b. Why did transportation normally mean permanent exile?
c. Of what crime had these labourers been found guilty?
d. How 'popular' was the verdict found on the Dorchester Weavers?
e. Why were agricultural workers slow to form a trade union?

8a. Meeting of the Trade Unionists at Copenhagen Fields, 21st April 1834, to carry a petition to the king for a remission of the sentences passed on the Dorchester labourers

8b. Farm workers at their sixth annual Trade Union demonstration at Yeovil, Whit Monday, 1877

29 Parliament Against
Trade Unionism, 1799

8 April: Sir John Anderson brought up a Report of a Select Committee, to whom the Petition of the master millwrights was referred. The substance of the Report was that there existed among the journeymen millwrights, within certain districts in and about the metropolis, a combination which was dangerous to the public, and which the masters had not sufficient power to repress.

The Report being read, Sir John Anderson moved 'That leave be given to bring in a Bill to prevent unlawful combination of workmen employed in the millwright business, and to enable the magistrates to regulate their wages within certain limits.'

Mr. Wilberforce said he did not object to the principle of this motion . . . but he [asked] whether it might not be advisable to extend the principle of this motion, and make it general against combinations of all workmen. These combinations he regarded as a general disease in our society.

17 June: Mr. Chancellor Pitt said it was his intention to endeavour to provide a remedy to an evil of very considerable magnitude; he meant that of unlawful combination among workmen in general — a practice which had become much too general, and was likely, if not checked, to produce very serious mischief. He could not state particularly the nature of the Bill which he intended to move for leave to bring in; but it would be modelled in some respect on that of the Bill for regulating the conduct of the paper manufacturers . . . He then moved that leave be given to bring in a Bill to prevent unlawful combinations of workmen.

Debate in the House of Commons, 1799, *Debrett*, vols. LIII–LIV.

Comment

Trade unions were one result of the Industrial Revolution.

These early unions were local, because of the difficulties of communication; they were confined to one craft because of the common problems of people in that craft.

In 1799 the antagonism against trade unions and the fear of revolution made the Government pass the Combination Acts. This extract shows the antagonism of some politicians towards trade unions, and also shows how Pitt, the Prime Minister, took the attack away from one named union to all unions.

Questions

a. Who had formed a 'combination'? Where?
b. What evidence is there that the first trade unions were: (i) local in character; (ii) each confined to members of one craft?
c. Which three people mentioned in the extract thought that unions were a danger?
d. What did Sir John Anderson propose?
e. Show that Wilberforce was anxious to extend the attack.
f. What did Pitt propose?
g. What evidence is there that the number of trade unions was increasing?
h. Write a paragraph on the Combination Acts.

30 Employers Unite Against Unions

Perhaps you have known of instances . . . in which employers have dictated terms to the employed, which interfere with their rights as workmen? — Yes, I have known a great many instances of that kind . . . There was a contention . . . at Stockport, in the beginning of 1829, about wages; and . . . a strike was the consequence; and the masters of Hyde thought proper to interfere; . . . in their own words, as published and placarded they say —

'We, the . . . manufacturers of Hyde, Staley Bridge, Dukinfield, and the neighbourhood, having observed . . . distress of the operatives of Stockport, instigated by evil-designing persons to [strike] and being informed that this distress is prolonged by assistance being rendered by our work-people to the turn-outs (= strikers) in that town, do hereby agree to abate ten per cent every fortnight . . . the wages of . . . our . . . hands who . . . refuse to sign a declaration that they will not . . . become members of any combination interfering with the free exercise of individual labour; or . . . contribute to the support of any turn-outs, on pain of forfeiting a fortnight's wages, should they be found so doing.'

Immediately afterwards, . . . an agreement was offered by the masters . . .; the operatives were to sign [as follows], or not be employed; . . . (The following document was then put in, and read:)

'We, the undersigned, agree with Messrs. —— that we will work for them on the following terms: 'We declare that we do not belong to . . . the 'Union', or any other society . . . which has for its object any interference with the rules laid down for the government of mills. 'We agree with our . . . masters, that we will not become members of . . . any such society while . . . in our present employ. 'We will not . . . subscribe or contribute to any such society, or to any turn-out hands whatsoever. 'And if we are discovered to act contrary to the above agreement, each of us so offending will forfeit a sum equal to a fortnight's wages . . .'

Evidence before a Select Committee, Parliamentary Papers, 1831–2, xv, pp. 28–30.

Comment

Although the legal position of trade unions had been changed by the Acts of 1824 and 1825, manufacturers were still opposed to their formation, and many magistrates managed to find a way of making them seem illegal.

This extract shows that combinations of manufacturers existed, and that those at Hyde, etc., were anxious to break a strike (a 'turn-out') at Stockport. The workmen at Hyde had been supporting the strikers, but would now have to suffer a wage reduction if they formed a union or supported a strike.

Questions

a. How had workers at Hyde helped strikers at Stockport?

b. How were the masters going to stop this?

c. Why, do you think, did the 'masters of Hyde' think it 'proper to interfere' in the strike at Stockport?

d. What punishment was proposed?

e. What evidence is there in the document that the manufacturers were thinking of the interests of the workpeople?

f. How was the workman punished if he refused to sign the document?

g. When were Combination Acts repealed?

h. How does (i) Plate 8, (ii) this extract, show that the repeal of the Combination Acts had little effect?

31 The Strike That Failed

There was no eagerness for a strike, for there were no defensive resources. The 'tommy' shops[1] would close . . . There were no co-operative societies . . . with little saved-up balances to the name of each member. The union had no reserve funds. . . . So methods of conciliation were resorted to . . . On March 20, 1844, the men sent a letter to the owners asking them . . . to receive a deputation from the Miners' Association. There was no reply of any sort.

In 1844 the men . . . left their work in April; and immediate steps were taken to fill the place left vacant. Men were brought from Wales . . ., under much better terms than those which had been refused to the men on the spot. Then came the evictions. The coalowners are the proprietors of the cottages in which the pitmen live. Occupancy can . . . be terminated with the cessation of employment, and eviction means . . . the throwing out of the people . . . into the village street.

Henry Barrass, eighty years of age, and his wife, aged seventy-five, were turned out into the rain and the night. The men saw windows and doors being broken to pieces in order that the meagre household goods . . . which had been gathered together with much paid and self-denial, might be thrown out into the street. There was no possibility of finding house accommodation for . . . those who had been evicted. The workhouses, too, were closed against the strikers. 'Starvation had to be endured', [for] twenty-six weeks, during which no word of any sort could be obtained from the employers . . .

Just as the cause might be, it was not at that time destined to prevail. . . . The mine-owners won 'hands down', . . . by treating the men as if they did not exist, except when their furniture was to be cast out of the cottages.

[1] Shops owned by the company.

Aaron Watson, *The Life of Thomas Burt*, 1908.

Comment

This is an extract from the biography of Thomas Burt, one of the first working-class men to be elected to Parliament. The treatment of working men by the mine owners was one of the main reasons why Burt became first a union leader and then a politician.

The owners here did not fight the union, as they had done at Tolpuddle. They simply ignored it; and when the men withdrew their labour, the owners brought in labour from elsewhere. In a country with a rapidly growing population, Irish immigration, railways (Document 12) and frequent depression (Document 28), labour was a mobile factor.

Questions

a. Give three reasons why there 'was no eagerness for a strike'.
b. What is meant by a 'tommy' shop? How would a co-operative society have helped the strikers, whereas the 'tommy' shop did not?
c. How did the owners treat the letter written on 20th March?
d. Why did the employers offer the Welsh better conditions than those they had refused to the local men?
e. Who owned the miners' cottages? How did this affect the strikers?
f. How long did the strike last? Who won?
g. Give the reasons why the men had to go back on the owners' terms.
h. How does this document help to explain class bitterness in some areas?

32 A New Attitude Towards Trade Unionism

The objects of trade unions are . . . twofold:

1. *First* Those of a friendly . . . society — to afford relief to the members of the union . . . incapacitated . . . by accident or sickness; to allow a sum for the funeral expenses of the members and their wives; and sometimes to provide superannuation allowances for members [in] old age.

2. *Secondly* Those of a trade society proper — viz. to watch over . . . the interests of the working classes . . . and especially to protect them against the . . . advantage which the command of a large capital is supposed by them to give to the employers . . .

The objects last referred to are the main objects . . . It is, however, found desirable . . . to combine with these objects the functions of a friendly . . . society. Additional members and additional funds are thus obtained; and the hold which the society has over its members is strengthened [since] any member who subjects himself to expulsion for disobedience to the orders of the union . . . would thereby forfeit the superannuation and other benefits to which he would be entitled.

The agency through which the trade unions [work is] direct and indirect. The direct agency is by means of what is termed a 'strike', the ultimate sanction. . . .

It does not appear . . . that the disposition to strike . . . is in itself the [result] of unionism, or that the frequency of strikes increases in proportion to the strength of the union. It is, indeed, affirmed by the . . . unions that the effect of the established societies is to diminish the frequency, and certainly the disorder, of strikes; . . . its organisation is powerful [so obtains] the concession demanded without recourse to a strike.

Report of Royal Commission 1867–9, Parliamentary Papers, 1868–9, XXXI.

Comment

The period after 1870 saw a changing attitude towards trade unionism. In part, this was due to the work of the leaders of the craft unions which had been formed after the failure of Owen's Grand National Union. The Amalgamated Society of Engineers is the classic example. These unions gave evidence to this committee.

The leaders of these 'model' unions, national in scope thanks to improved communications, were moderate men, who ran disciplined unions. Most of the leaders lived in London (the communications centre of the country), and worked with each other to try and influence politicians, writers and others, and, through them, public opinion. They tried to show that trade unionism was a reasonable, not a revolutionary, development.

Questions

a. What is a 'friendly society'? What benefits did members derive?
b. Why could skilled workmen afford to pay higher union fees than unskilled workmen? What benefits did these fees bring?
c. What is the second (and main) aim of a union?
d. Why would a workman not willingly disobey the orders of his union?
e. Did unionism lead to strikes? Why?
f. Show that this extract did not apply to unskilled labourers. (Wages, employment, union.)
g. '... a strike ... the ultimate sanction ...' What is meant by this? What would happen in negotiations if the workers did not have this sanction?
h. What evidence is there that public opinion was now more favourable to trade unions?

9a. Lake Vyrnwy was begun in 1881. It was then Liverpool's main source of water.

9b. One of Watt's beam engines which was used to help pump water from Wales to Birmingham

Comment

The rapid development of new towns (Document 13) where there was little or no local government (Documents 5 and 13) had resulted in the creation of unhealthy towns (Plate 4a). The high mortality rates (Document 21) in these towns led to demands for various reforms.

Chadwick had shown (Document 16) that *laissez-faire* was largely responsible for the state of the towns. He showed that when people combined they could have plenty of clean water, and an adequate gas supply. This combining of society for such purpose has been called 'Gas and Water Socialism'.

People in a town can provide themselves with these and other amenities by way of their local council. The development of local government was a major feature of the period 1830–70.

Questions

a. What is the 'lake' in Plate 9a?
b. Where did people obtain water in small villages? Why was this not possible in towns like Birmingham, Manchester and Liverpool?
c. How did the inhabitants of large towns pay for their water supply?
d. What other amenities, apart from gas and water, does your local authority provide now?

33 Criticisms of the Unreformed Corporations

In general, corporate funds are partially applied to municipal purposes, such as the preservation of the peace by an efficient police . . . or lighting the town; . . . they are frequently expended in feasting, and in paying the salaries of unimportant officers. In some cases, in which the funds are expended on public purposes, such as building public works, . . . an expense has been incurred . . . beyond what would be necessary if due care had been taken. These abuses often originate in negligence . . . but more frequently in the opportunity afforded . . . of obliging members of their own body, or the friends and relations of such members.

Some Corporations consider that their property has been vested in them solely as trustees for the public; but, in most cases, this truth is acknowledged only when forced on their attention, . . . and is continually forgotten. . . .

. . . There prevails amongst the inhabitants of a great majority of the incorporated towns a general, and, in our opinion, a just dissatisfaction with their municipal institutions; a distrust of the self-elected municipal councils, whose powers are subject to no popular control, and whose acts and proceedings being secret, are unchecked by the influence of public opinion; . . . a discontent under the burthens of local taxation, while revenues that ought to be applied for the public advantage are diverted from their legitimate use, and are sometimes wastefully bestowed for the benefit of individuals, sometimes squandered for purposes injurious to the character and morals of the people.

Royal Commission on Municipal Corporation 1835, Parliamentary Papers, 1835, XXIII.

Comment

This is an extract from the report of the Royal Commission appointed by the Whig Government (1831-5) to examine the government of the 250 or so incorporated boroughs. In 1835 the Commission found that the existing boroughs had a medieval type of local government with little or no professional paid staff.

The Commission did not examine the government of non-corporate towns, i.e. towns which had no Royal Charter, so the Commission did not examine the government of, say, Manchester.

The Commissioners were sent out by the Whigs. The majority were young barristers, and they held democratic views. They were eager to find fault with what they saw and one Commissioner, Sir Francis Palgrave, signed a Minority Report complaining of the violence of the criticism. However, there is no doubt that the existing structure of local government was in need of overhaul in the 1830s.

Questions

a. What is an incorporated town? (See Documents 5 and 14.)
b. Why did the Commissioners not visit the new industrial towns?
c. Members of some corporations were accused of being corrupt. Paragraph 1 gives two ways in which they used their position for their own benefit. What were they?
d. How did members of some corporations spend the money they received from corporate property?
e. How can a group be self-elected? Who would choose the person to fill a vacancy in such a corporation?
f. What evidence is there in this extract that the Commissioners were 'democratic' in their outlook?
g. What evidence is there of demand for Municipal Reform?
h. Why did the Reform Act (1832) lead to demand for Municipal Reform?

34 Part of the Municipal Corporations Act, 1835

Every male person of full age who shall have occupied any house ... or shop within any Borough during that year and the whole of each of the two preceding years, and shall have been an inhabitant householder within the said Borough, or within seven miles of the said Borough, shall be a burgess of such Borough: [if] he shall have been rated in respect of such premises so occupied by him ...

In every Borough shall be elected one person, called 'The Mayor' ...; a certain number of persons called 'Aldermen' ...; a certain number of other persons called 'The Councillors' ... The number to be elected Aldermen shall be one third of the number to be elected Councillors; the Council ... shall elect from the Councillors, or from the persons qualified to be Councillors, the Aldermen of such Borough.

It may be expedient that the powers now vested in the watching, regulating, supplying with water, and improving certain Boroughs, or certain parts thereof, should be transferred to the Councils of such Boroughs respectively; the Trustees appointed by virtue of any such Act of Parliament may transfer, in writing under their hands and seals, all the powers vested in them to the said Body Corporate of such Borough.

The Council shall immediately after their first election, appoint a sufficient number of their own Body, called the Watch Committee ...; such Watch Committee shall appoint a sufficient number of men ... to act as Constables for preserving the peace by day and night.

Statutes of the Realm, 5 & 6 William IV, c. 76.

Comment

This is an extract from the Municipal Reform Act, 1835. Here, as in national politics, property was the criterion; the £10 householder had a vote after 1832, and the ratepayer was given a vote in local elections after 1835.

The Act only applied to 178 towns which had Royal Charters. However, the Act created a framework under which other towns could have the Act extended to them.

Nor did the Act try to deal with the social problems of both old and new towns in the matter of sanitation, housing, etc. The Act reformed institutions but laid few obligations on people. It cost little to administer.

Questions

a. Who would become a burgess?
b. How did the Act help the new middle classes? Compare their civic position before and after this Act.
c. Who elected the councillors?
d. Who elected: (i) the aldermen; (ii) the Mayor?
e. What powers might a council have transferred? (See Documents 14 and 16 for Private Acts.)
f. What does paragraph 4 tell us about: (i) the ideas of those who passed the Act; (ii) their supporters?
g. 'This Act did nothing for the lower classes.' What evidence does this extract offer to support this view?
h. Why would the abuses described in Document 33 not occur so easily after the passing of this Act? (Think of the number of voters, frequency of elections and publicity.)

35 The Evolution
of Active Government

A new ideal arose. Its purpose was to forsake the . . . 'laissez-faire' of the eighteenth century, and adopt collectivism; [or] what was called 'socialism'. . . .

From the Reform Bill of 1832 we can date . . . an enormous improvement in the health of the people. This is . . . because it . . . produced three measures which . . . the people demanded: *first*, the . . . Factory Act of 1833, . . .; *secondly*, the Poor Law Amendment Act of 1834, and . . . the . . . Poor Law Commission, the first central board concerned with public health . . . *Thirdly* came in 1835 the Municipal Corporations Act, which readjusted the administrative areas of the boroughs. From these three Acts was to grow up . . . almost the whole of the modern statutory services on behalf of the health of the people.

. . . In 1859 [the Board] was succeeded partly by the Home Office and partly by the Privy Council; a medical department was established with Simon as medical officer and a staff of . . . medical inspectors, who produced the . . . series of reports on epidemics, pulmonary diseases, infant mortality, food-supply, housing, sanitary [conditions], and vaccination. Thus Simon was the creator of the present system.

Ten years later, in 1869, a Royal Commission, . . . inspired by Rumsey and a number of medical and social workers, . . . recommended that 'the present fragmentary and confused sanitary legislation should be consolidated'. They proposed, in fact, for the first time, a Ministry of Health; but the case miscarried and the Local Government Board was created in 1871.

Sir George Newman, *The Rise of Preventive Medicine.*

Comment

The author of this extract, Sir George Newman, a successor of Sir John Simon (paragraph 3), is giving an account of the way in which national and local government slowly evolved.

The three Acts mentioned in paragraph 2 had far wider effects than was originally intended — one led to more inspection in more fields (sanitary, housing, food and drugs, etc.), another led to the establishment of other centralised departments (education, local government, etc.), and the reform of local government created bodies which were capable of applying new laws.

The creation of the Local Government Board in 1871 was a landmark in the evolution of modern society. After this there was adequate supervision at the centre to make sure the laws were carried out, and an accepted connection between local government and public health.

Questions

a. What is meant by *laissez-faire*? How did such a policy lead to the conditions described in Document 14?

b. What is meant here by 'socialism'? How does the building of a municipal water-works (Document 16) help us to understand 'collectivism'?

c. Why was the Poor Law Commission anxious to improve conditions (Document 15)?

d. Why did the appointment of Medical Officers lead to a demand for improved sanitary legislation?

e. What work did the Board of Health do from 1859 to 1869?

f. What did some reformers hope for in 1870? When was the local Government Board created?

g. There was little change in the powers of local councils from 1835 to 1871, yet Sir George Newman claims that these were important years. Why?

h. How did the 'new ideal' affect: (i) the need for educational reform; (ii) taxation; (iii) the increase in the number of professional people? (Document 24).

36 The Argument Against
Laissez-faire

. . . Without these laws, [would] the suffering classes have been delivered . . . from the condition they were in? . . . No one considering the facts can have any doubt as to the answer to this question. Left to itself, . . . a degraded population perpetuates . . . itself. Read any of the authorised accounts, given before royal or parliamentary commissions, of the state of the labourers . . . as they were in our great industries before the law was . . . brought to bear on them . . . Ask yourself what chance there was of a generation, born and bred under such conditions, ever contracting out of them. Given a certain standard of . . . well-being, people may be trusted not to sell their labour, or the labour of their children, on [low] terms . . . But with large masses of our population . . . there was no such standard. There was nothing on their part, in the way either of self-respect or established demand for comforts, to prevent them from working and living, or from putting their children to work and live, in a way in which no one who is to be a healthy and free citizen can work and live. No doubt there were many high-minded employers who did their best for their workpeople . . . but they could not prevent less scrupulous hirers of labour from hiring it on the cheapest terms. Either the standard of well-being . . . of labour must prevent them from selling their labour under those conditions, or the law must prevent it. With a population such as ours was forty years ago, and still largely is, the law must prevent it . . . [until] the sellers will be in a state to prevent it for themselves.

T. H. Green, *Lecture on Liberal Legislation*, ed. 1888.

Comment

The growth of government interference at both national and local level was welcomed by Sir George Newman (Document 35) and by professional and social workers. This interference was against the principle of *laissez-faire* as understood by Senior (Document 18) and the principle of self-help developed by Samuel Smiles (Document 17).

The author of this extract, T. H. Green, was a lecturer on political ideas, an admirer of Bright (Document 43), and an enemy of *laissez-faire*, as the extract shows. He explains that the application of *laissez-faire* might benefit a minority (factory owners, property owners, etc.), but was harmful to the majority (workers, slum dwellers, etc.). This conclusion led him to question the meaning of freedom; he concluded that the slum dweller and the factory children were not free. Therefore, since freedom was desirable, legislation must be passed to create freedom for the less fortunate.

Questions

a. In what ways were many workers 'suffering' before the Factory Act of 1833? (See Document 22.)

b. How did 'these laws' help to improve conditions?

c. Read again Document 21. Why did such findings require legislation?

d. We have today a 'certain standard of well-being'. Do you agree that present-day parents could be 'trusted not to sell the labour of their children' as cheaply as did parents in the early 19th century?

e. Why did the existence of some 'less scrupulous' factory owners require a law affecting all factories? (See Document 20.)

f. The extract deals with Factory Acts. Name three other fields in which the law helped to improve conditions of life for the working classes. (See Document 14.)

g. Why did Factory Acts and other laws lead to a larger Civil Service?

h. How would Smiles (Document 17) have answered the author of this extract? Why was 'Reform' a slow process?

PEEL'S CHEAP BREAD SHOP.

OPENED JANUARY 22, 1846.

10a

10b   NOT SO *VERY* UNREASONABLE!!! EH?

Comment

Two movements dominated the political scene from 1838 to 1850 One, the Anti-Corn Law League, succeeded (Plate 10a); the other, the Chartist movement (Plate 10b), failed.

The Corn Laws had been passed by the Tory Government in 1815, so interfering with Free Trade (Document 37). It was the Tories, Huskisson, Peel and Gladstone, who were mainly responsible for the repeal of these laws. Peel had seen the advantage of Free Trade; the middle-class industrialists, such as Cobden (Document 38), argued the case against the Corn Law and convinced Peel. In January 1846 he abolished the Corn Laws but split the Tory Party (Document 39).

The Chartist Movement (Document 28) received little support in Parliament. Its aims were not as easy to understand as was the cry of 'cheap bread', so it received less popular support than the Anti-Corn Law League. Prime Minister Lord John Russell could afford to allow the petition to be presented.

Questions

a. Why is 'R. Peel' the name of the cheap bread shop? Who was Russell?
b. Why was this 'shop' opened in January 1846?
c. What is 'the Charter'? Why is it such a huge roll?
d. Why did many people support the cry 'cheap bread', and few supported the cry 'the Charter'?

37 Free Trade Benefits Everyone

. . . Your Committee are satisfied that the skill, enterprise, and capital of British merchants . . . require only an open and [free] field for exertion; and that the most valuable boon that can be conferred on them is unlimited freedom . . .

Your Committee . . . call the observation of the House to the . . . complexity of the laws under which the commerce of the country is regulated . . . These laws amount to upwards of 2,000; . . . the British merchant (his transactions being plain and simple) . . . is frequently reduced to . . . resorting to the services of professional advisers, to ascertain what he may . . . do and what he must avoid, before he is able to embark on his commercial adventures.

It can scarcely be denied that they have a tendency to cramp the operations of commerce and to impede the growth of opulence . . .

Commerce . . . must be a source of reciprocal amity between nations, and an interchange of productions, to promote the industry, the wealth, and the happiness of mankind.

Your Committee are [aware] that at once to abandon the . . . system would be . . . dangerous . . . They feel that gradual . . . approximation to a sounder system . . . may be . . . recommended, with a view to the interests of the country [and] of surrounding nations. It is not to prohibitions and protections we are indebted for our commercial greatness . . .; these, like every . . . blessing we enjoy, are the effects of the free principles of the constitution under which we live . . . [which] by holding out the most splendid rewards to successful industry . . . has . . . excited the efforts, encouraged the genius, and called into action all the powers of an aspiring, enlightened, and enterprising people.

Report by Select Committee of House of Commons, 18th July 1820, Hansard, v, App. cxxx–cx/xi.

Comment

One of the main aims of commercial policy had been to limit imports and increase exports. Imports could be limited by encouraging new industries to develop here, which would lead to decreased imports of some products; import taxes (tariffs or duties) would increase the price of the import, and make it more costly, so that less of it would be bought. The document shows how many and complex were the laws governing trade in 1820.

The older (or Protectionist) view had been attacked by Adam Smith in *The Wealth of Nations*.

By 1820 Adam Smith's arguments had gained ground, London merchants asked Parliament to end the existing commercial restrictions; the House of Commons had set up a Select Committee to look into their arguments. This is an extract from the Committee's Report.

Questions

a. Britain had been first in the Industrial Revolution. Why should the Committee be satisfied that 'the skill, enterprise and capital of British merchants require only an open and free field for exertion'?

b. How many laws were there 'under which the commerce of the country is regulated'?

c. How did this affect foreign trade?

d. How does the final sentence help us to understand the meaning of *laissez-faire*?

e. Show that the supporters of Free Trade believed that it would increase the nation's wealth.

f. Show how it might lead to greater chance of world peace.

g. The Committee was against a sudden change of policy. Why?

h. Which part of the document foreshadows the work of Huskisson (1822–7), Peel (1841–6) and Gladstone (1853–60)?

38 Cobden on Corn Laws

In the first place, we want Free Trade in corn, because we think it just; because we believe that, if we obtain that, we shall get rid of all other monopolies without any trouble. We require it at the natural price of the world's market, whether it becomes dearer with free trade — or whether it is cheaper, it matters not, provided the people . . . have it at its natural price, and every source of supply is freely opened, as nature and nature's God intended it to be; we do not believe that Free Trade in corn will injure the farmer.

Neither do we believe it will injure the farm-labourer. We think it will enlarge the market for his labour, and give him an opportunity of finding employment, not only on the soil (by the improvements which agriculturists must adopt) but that there will also be a general rise in wages from the increased demand for employment in the . . . towns. We do not expect that it will injure the land-owner, provided he [thinks only of] his pecuniary interest in the matter; we have no doubt it will interfere with his political despotism . . . [see Document 41].

We believe that Free Trade will increase the demand for labour of every kind, not merely of the mechanical classes and those engaged in laborious bodily occupations, but for clerks, shopmen and ware-housemen, giving employment to all those youths whom you are so desirous of setting out in the world . . . Finally, we believe that Free Trade will not diminish, but, on the contrary, increase the Queen's revenue.

Cobden, *Speeches*, 1870.

Comment

The middle classes were given the vote in 1832 (Document 42), and most voted Whig, partly because it was the Whigs who had given them the vote, partly because the Tory Anglicans aroused the opposition of the Non-Conformist middle classes more than did the Low Church and Non-Conformist Whigs. However, the newly enfranchised middle classes soon found that their Whig party had less idea of commercial and industrial progress than the Tories as represented by Gladstone and Peel.

The industrial middle classes therefore founded the Anti-Corn Law League to spread ideas of Free Trade as well as to abolish the Corn Laws, imposed in 1815 to help the farmer and landowner. The League had its headquarters in Manchester, one of the new towns, and was led by Cobden and Bright, members of the middle classes. They took advantage of new developments, such as the railway and Penny Post, to spread their idea that the future greatness of the country lay in its industrial and not in its agricultural development.

Questions

a. The speaker is Cobden. What does he mean when he says 'we'?

b. What is a monopoly? Who, after the Corn Laws (1815), had a monopoly of the British Corn Market?

c. Why was corn not being sold at its 'natural price'?

d. '.... by the improvements ...' Why would Free Trade compel farmers to adopt new methods?

e. How would Free Trade affect the farm labourers?

f. How would it affect the demand for labour in general? (See also Document 23.)

g. Why was Cobden supported by: (i) industrialists; (ii) the working classes?

h. How did the Anti-Corn Law League use: (i) the Penny Post; (ii) the railways?

39 Disraeli Leads the Opposition, 1846

. . . This is a question of displacing the labour that produces corn to permit the entrance of corn produced by foreign labour. Will that displaced labour find employment? The Secretary of State says that England is no longer an agricultural country . . . I doubt whether England is a greater commercial country now than she has been at other periods . . . If you look to the general distribution of labour in England you will find she may be less of a manufacturing country now than she has been [when] manufacturing industry was more scattered over the country . . . You have, no doubt, now a gigantic development of manufacturing skill in a particular county, which has been a great source of public wealth. But it is confined to one county; and now Ministers tell us we must change our whole system, in favour of one county. What are the resources of this industry to employ . . . the people [if] the great depression in agriculture occurs — in fact from 3,500,000 to 4,000,000 people? Assume that the workshop of the world principle is carried into effect [and] a gigantic industry is doubled, you would only find increased employment for 300,000 of your population. I think we have pretty good grounds for anticipating social misery and political disaster.

(He attacks Peel for betraying the Protectionist cause.)

· . . . Gentlemen . . . profess doctrines contrary to those of these new economists. They place themselves at the head of [the Tory] party, and clamber into power . . . We trusted to one who at this moment governs England . . . Suddenly, the announcement . . . [of] another change, which only a few months before [Peel] had described as a 'social revolution'. And how was this announcement made? It was announced through the columns of [The Times].

Hansard, 3, LXXXVI, 665–79.

Comment

The Anti-Corn Law League had developed to support Free Trade in general and the Repeal of the Corn Laws in particular. Peel had supported Free Trade in general but opposed the Anti-Corn Law League. By 1845 he had become convinced of the need for Repeal, and in a sense was betraying the interests of the farming community who had put him in power.

Disraeli led the opposition to Repeal. He disliked Peel, who had 'betrayed the Protestant cause' in 1829, and had not offered Disraeli a position in the Government (1841–6).

In this extract he argues that Repeal will mean social misery, i.e. unemployment, for millions. We know that this was not so in the period up to 1870.

Questions

a. Who would be displaced if there were Free Trade in corn? What had Cobden to say about this (Document 38)?
b. Why did Disraeli think that England was less of a manufacturing country than she had been? Do you think he was right?
c. Which 'particular county' is Disraeli speaking of? Where did the 'new economists' have their headquarters?
d. How many farm workers would lose their jobs, according to this extract? How many of them would find jobs in the cotton industry?
e. Disraeli anticipated 'social misery'. How does the evidence of Giffen (Document 23) and Caird (Document 40) show that he was wrong in the period up to 1870?
f. What had Peel described as a 'social revolution'? What was Peel's attitude towards this revolution in 1845?
g. Disraeli also anticipated 'political disaster'. For which politician, and for which party, was this true?
h. Write a brief account of Peel's Free Trade Budgets. When were the Corn Laws repealed?

40 How Farmers Can Prosper under Free Trade

More land should be laid to grass, or a greater extent devoted to the production of meat and vegetables [and], as a result of better cultivation there would be little diminution in the production of corn [because of] a larger acreage return.

Experience shows that this change would not prove injurious to the labourer. Green crops require more labour than corn. It is in the strictly corn districts of the south and east that the labourer's condition is most depressed. The dairy lands of North Wilts, Gloucester and Aylesbury afford better wages than the corn districts of the same counties, Salisbury Plain and the Chiltern hills.

[There is an] advantage to the landlord, who receives, and to the tenant who pays rent, of cultivating the produce which has a tendency to increase in value in this country. With the present prices, and the knowledge that the rich corn provinces of the continent are open to us, and are daily becoming more accessible by the extension of railway and steam navigation, there seems good reason to anticipate the permanence of a low range of prices. The safe course for the English agriculturist is to try, by increasing his live stock, to render himself less dependent on corn, while he at the same time enriches his farm by their manure and is thus able to grow heavier crops at less cost.

J. Caird, *English Agriculture in 1850–1*, 1852.

Comment

Disraeli had expressed the fears of English farmers (Document 39); Cobden had said that the farmer had nothing to fear from Free Trade (Document 38). In fact they were both right. Farmers who continued to grow mainly wheat suffered from falling prices. By 1850 imports of wheat had doubled in quantity, and the price of wheat had halved. However, the price of other products was rising, due to increased demand. Butter, cheese, eggs and meat became part of the diet of the population. This growing population was prosperous (Documents 23 and 24) and the farmer could distribute his produce because of the railway (Document 12).

James Caird, the author of this extract, was a farmer. His pamphlet, *High Farming* (1849), caused *The Times* to appoint him a 'commissioner' into English farming. His findings and recommendations are given in this extract.

Questions

a. What does he suggest English farmers should produce?

b. Why would there be only 'little diminution in production of corn'?

c. How had farm labourers been affected by Free Trade: (i) in the South and East; (ii) in Gloucester?

d. Why were wheat prices falling? Did the author expect this fall to continue?

e. How would dairy farming affect: (i) the tenant; (ii) the landowner?

f. How would an increase in livestock affect the quality of arable land?

g. Why did some products have 'a tendency to increase in value in this country'?

h. How did Britain (i) gain, (ii) lose, by the development of the steamship?

A LEAP IN THE DARK.

Comment

Old Sarum (Plate 11a) was the symbol of the old Parliamentary system (Document 41). It had been an inhabited town and had been justified in having a member of Parliament. By 1800 it was no longer a town — but still had a member of Parliament. 'There were many such boroughs', as Southey shows (Document 41).

The new towns and the new wealth demanded reform, and got some in 1832 (Document 42). Demands for further reform came from the Chartists (Document 28 and Plate 10b) from 1838 onwards. These demands were met by the Reform of 1867. As Plate 11b shows, many people were uncertain as to the result of this reform (Document 43) in which many working-class men were given the vote.

Questions

a. Why was there an M.P. for Old Sarum? Who elected this member?
b. When did 'industrial towns as . . . Birmingham' gain representation in Parliament?
c. Through what barrier is Britannia crashing, August 1867? Who is the horse? (See Document 43.)
d. How does Plate 11b show that the 'Reform' worried some people (Document 43)?

11a. Old Sarum, Wiltshire. What had been the borough of Sarum was now no more than a field of which the owner was the sole elector of a Member of Parliament. There were many such 'rotten boroughs' while industrial towns such as Manchester and Birmingham were without any representation.

41 The Corrupt Parliamentary System

. . . Some seats are private property; the right of voting belongs to a few householders . . . and . . . these votes are commanded by the owner of the estate. The fewer they are, the more easily they are managed. [A] great part of a borough in the west . . . was consumed some years ago by fire, and the lord of the manor would not suffer the houses to be rebuilt for this reason. If such an estate is to be sold, it is advertised as carrying . . . the power of returning two members. Government hold many of these boroughs, and individuals buy others. . . . In this manner are a majority of the members returned.

. . . Where the number of voters is greater, . . . the business is more difficult, and . . . expensive. The candidate . . . must deal individually with the constituents, who sell themselves to the highest bidder. Remember that an oath against bribery is required! A common mode of evading the . . . oath is . . . a wager. 'I will bet so much,' says the agent of the candidate, 'that you do not vote for us.' 'Done,' says the voter . . . — goes [to vote] and returns to receive the money, not as the price of his suffrage, but as the bet . . . At Aylesbury a bowl of guineas stood . . . in the committee-room, and the voters were helped out of it. The price of votes varies according to their number. In some places it is as low as forty shillings, in others . . . it is thirty pounds. 'Thirty pounds,' said the apothecary . . . 'is the price of an Ilchester voter.' When asked how he came to know the sum . . . he replied that . . . his bills were paid at election times with the money.

R. Southey, *Letters from England*, 1807.

Comment

There are three main headings under which the electoral system should be studied. Many of the *constituencies* (Plate 11a) were controlled either by the owner of the estate or by the Government. The *franchise* varied from universal male franchise (in Preston) to the examples given in this document.

In many constituencies the owner would ensure the return of his own

Freedom & Purity of Election !!! Showing the Necessity of Reform in the Close Boroughs.

11c

candidates. Some constituencies had a wider franchise, and here *bribery* was practised. The cost of a seat was very high: Gladstone bought Newark for £5,000.

However, the system had to be changed because the House of Commons no longer represented the bulk of the people, who had move from the older centres of population to the new unrepresented towns (Sections 4 and 6). Nor had even the new wealthy middle classes the vote. It was for these that Macaulay spoke (Document 42).

Questions

a. Why could a seat in the House of Commons be 'private property'?

b. Why did the 'lord of the manor' not allow 'the houses to be re-built'? What does this tell us of elections in 1807? (See Plate 11a.)

c. Who, according to Southey, bought the boroughs?

d. What evidence is there in the document that there was no universal qualification for the vote?

e. Why did this make some constituencies more difficult to control?
An oath against bribery was required. Give three examples from the document of money bribes offered during elections.

g. Why did the lack of a secret ballot allow the owner of an estate to command votes?

h. Why did (i) the career of Younger Pitt, (ii) Britain's victory over Napoleon encourage some to think that the Old System was a good one?

42 Reform Will Prevent
Revolution — Macaulay, 1831

But, Sir, every argument which would induce me to oppose universal suffrage induces me to support the plan which is now before us. I am opposed to universal suffrage, because . . . it would produce a destructive revolution. I support this plan; I am sure it is our best security against a revolution.

. . . That we may exclude those whom it is necessary to exclude, we must admit those whom it may be safe to admit. At present we oppose the schemes of revolutionaries . . . with only one quarter of our proper force. We say . . . that it is not by mere numbers, but by property and intelligence, that the nation ought to be governed. Yet, saying this, we exclude . . . great masses of property and intelligence . . . We do more. We drive over to the side of revolution those whom we shut out from power.

. . . History is full of revolutions, produced by causes similar to those which are now operating in England. A portion of the community which had been of no account expands and becomes strong. It demands a place in the system, suited . . . to its present power. If this is granted, all is well. If this is refused, then comes the struggle between the young energy of one class and the ancient privileges of another. Such is the struggle which the middle classes in England are maintaining against an aristocracy, . . . or the owner of a ruined hovel, [who have] powers which are withheld from cities renowned . . . for the marvels of their wealth and of their industry.

Speech in House of Commons, 2nd March 1831.

Comment

When the Tory Government under Wellington was defeated in 1831, William IV asked Earl Grey, leader of the Whigs, to form a Government, though he had not won the election of 1830. Grey, anxious to keep in power, was pledged to a policy of Parliamentary Reform and proposed a modest Reform Bill through Lord John Russell.

A Radical Reformer.   A Whole Bill Reformer.   A bit by bit Reformer.   An Anti Reformer.

FOUR SPECIMENS OF THE POLITICAL PUBLICK.

11d

Macaulay argued that this was a good Bill, a Bill which would bring property owners into Parliament, a Bill which was not too revolutionary, a Bill which would cream off potential leaders of revolution such as France had had in 1830. Macaulay proved right; by giving a little to the rising middle classes, revolution was avoided.

Questions

a. What evidence is there in this extract that Macaulay, a Whig, supported Wellington, a Tory, in his opposition to complete democracy?

b. Why did they fear it?

c. Who were the new property owners that Macaulay wanted to get into Parliament?

d. Why would they be opposed to increased taxes, revolution and greater democracy?

e. Which cities were 'renowned'? Why were they unrepresented in Parliament?

f. The French middle classes had led the July Revolution (1830) and the Bourbons had lost the throne. How did Macaulay apply the lesson to England in 1831?

g. Why did the House of Lords oppose the Bill? (See Document 41.) How did Grey overcome their opposition?

h. Give the terms of the Reform Act, 1832.

113

43 Demand for Working-class Franchise, 1865

An Englishman, if he goes to the Cape, . . . to Australia, . . . to the Canadian Confederation, he can vote; it is only in his own country . . . that he is denied this right . . .

But perhaps our friends who oppose us will say, 'We do not fear elections and order. What we fear is this — the legislative results of this wide extension of the franchise.' I am ready to test it in any country by the results of legislation. I say, whether you go to South Africa, or to Australia, or to the British North American provinces, you will find that life and property are as secure, . . . that the laws are as merciful and just, that taxes are imposed and levied with as great equality . . . as [in] this country . . .

It is not democracy . . . that is the peril of this country. It was not democracy in 1832 that was the peril. It was the desperate antagonism of the class that then had power to the just claims and rights of the people. And at this moment, . . . I tell them that Conservatism — . . . be it Tory or be it Whig, is the true national peril which we have to face. They may dam the stream, they may keep back the waters, but the volume is ever increasing, and it descends with accelerated force, and the time will come when, . . . if wisdom does not take the place of folly, the waters will burst their banks, and these men, who fancy they are stemming this imaginary apparition of democracy, will be swept away by the resolute will of a united and determined people.

John Bright, speech at Birmingham, 18th Jan. 1865.

Comment

The demand for an extension of the franchise had been kept alive by the Chartists in the 1840s, but they had failed to win either popular or parliamentary support. In the 1860s the demand became louder, support for parliamentary reform came from a new group, the Radicals, led by John Bright. He used the same arguments as Macaulay (Document 42) that if the upper classes did not give way to the demands of the lower classes, revolution would surely follow.

The opponents come from both parties, as Bright shows, but in the end Disraeli, with the support of the more liberal Whigs, passed the Reform Act of 1867.

Questions

a. In which countries was there a more democratic system in 1865?
b. What were Bright's opponents afraid of?
c. What results had followed great democracy in other countries?
d. What evidence is there here, and in Document 42, that there was 'class antagonism'?
e. Show that opposition to such an extension came from both political parties.
f. What consequences did Bright foresee if the franchise was not extended?
g. Who opposed Gladstone's Reform Bill, 1866?
h. Give the terms of the Act of 1867.

44 The Ballot Act, 1872

... The ballot of each voter shall consist of ... a ballot paper showing the names ... of the candidates. Each ballot paper shall have a number printed on the back, and shall have attached a counterfoil with the same number printed on the face. At the time of voting, the ballot paper shall be marked on both sides with an official mark, and delivered to the voter within the polling station, and the number of such voter on the register of voters shall be marked on the counterfoil, and the voter having secretly marked his vote on the paper, and folded it up so as to conceal his vote, shall place it in a closed box in the presence of the officer presiding at the polling station (in this Act called 'the presiding officer') after having shown to him the official mark at the back.

Any ballot paper which has not on its back the official mark, or on which votes are given to more candidates than the voter is entitled to vote for, or on which anything, except the said number on the back, is written or marked by which the voter can be identified, shall be void and not counted.

After the close of the poll the ballot boxes shall be sealed up, so as to prevent the introduction of additional ballot papers, and shall be taken charge of by the returning officer, and that officer shall, in the presence of such agents, if any, of the candidates as may be in attendance, open the ballot boxes, and ascertain the result of the poll by counting the votes given to each candidate, and shall forthwith declare to be elected the candidates or candidate to whom the majority of votes have been given.

Statutes of the Realm, 35 & 36 Victoria, c. 33.

Comment

Borough elections have been described by Dickens and others, and illustrated by Hogarth. Drunkenness, violence and gangs of young and old following bands hired to play party tunes, were as much a feature of the election as the bribery spoken of in Document 41. All this finished with the Ballot Act of 1872, which ended voting in public.

The bribery, drink and gangs were only effective so long as the open system of voting lasted. Under this system the voter went to the hustings and in full view of his fellow townsmen announced to the Returning Officer his vote for so and so.

It was to prevent this public voting that the Chartists had asked for a secret ballot. In 1872 a Liberal Government passed the Ballot Act. There might still be chances of corruption, but they would be far fewer than formerly. Property owners might still throw tenants out if their favoured candidate did not win, but such action was illegal, and was not often tried.

From 1872 the election would be decided by the voter's own conscience and convictions.

Questions

a. What was on the front of each ballot paper? Does the paper show the name of the candidate's political party?

b. Why was the paper marked with an official mark?

c. What is the register of voters? Do you know where it is kept in your town?

d. Why is 'secretly' so important?

e. How was this 'secrecy' kept after the voter had marked his paper?

f. Which papers were not to be counted?

g. What did the Returning Officer do? How did each candidate ensure that the 'count' was conducted fairly?

h. How did this Act lessen the likelihood of the incidents described in Document 41?

Comment

One of the reasons for the poor quality of education was the shortage of good teachers (Documents 45 and 46). The 'monitorial system' was an attempt to overcome this shortage. One good teacher would show an assistant (monitor) a certain lesson. This monitor would then teach the lesson to a form of younger pupils. The class teacher (Plate 12b) came later.

The monitors were boys who had gone through the school, reached the top class (or form) and had shown more than average ability. They would teach only that which they had learned themselves. Usually this was material learned by heart; it was easy to see if a child had learned a poem, multiplication tables, spelling lists, catechism, etc.

Questions

a. Where is the teacher's desk (Plate 12a)? Why could one person not 'teach' all these children?
b. Why would discipline have to be very strict in this type of school?
c. Pick out five people who are 'assistants' or 'monitors'.
d. How do arrangements in this school (Plate 12b) differ from those in the monitorial school?

12a. A Victorian engraving of a monitorial school, the Royal Free School, Borough Road, London -

12b. Cable Street School, London, 1908. Notice how conditions have improved since the monitorial school. The teacher is trying to give individual attention to his pupils.

45 Education in
the Early 19th Century

There were very few schools, and many of the teachers could not have passed our present Board Schools' Sixth standard. Some taught nothing but reading and spelling, or knitting and sewing; others only reading and writing from printed copies (not being able to write themselves so well). A few taught arithmetic as well, but a grammar, geography, or history were scarcely ever seen in a school . . . A few of the sons of the middle class learnt writing and arithmetic, but very few others learnt anything but reading. Large numbers never entered the door of a schoolhouse — having to work at something when they arrived at school age . . . Writing was looked upon . . . as a . . . luxury for the rich only, and never likely to be wanted by their sons and daughters. A person who was a good reader of the newspaper, and could talk about various wars, battles, and sieges, was looked up to by the people, and said to be a 'great scholar' and 'a far-learned man'. There were few school books, and those were of a poor kind, the tax or duty on paper . . . causing them to be very high in price. Newspapers were scarce and dear; very few could read them.

There were no libraries for the people, who had no access even to the few books there were; and the house that had a family Bible, hymn-book, prayer-book, or catechism, the 'Pilgrim's Progress', or 'News from the Invisible World', together with a sheet almanack nailed against the wall, was considered well furnished with literature.

Joseph Lawson, *Progress in Pudsey*, 1887.

Comment

This is an extract from the recollections of Joseph Lawson, written in 1887. He called his book *Progress in Pudsey* because he was aware of the great changes that had taken place in the years since 1820.

Most children never went to school, some because their parents sent them to work, some because their parents could not afford to pay even 2*d.* per week. Not until attendance was made compulsory would all children go to school.

12c. The Royal Freemason's School for 'female children', Wandsworth Common, opened on 2nd August 1852

The poor quality of the teachers was mainly due to the absence of any teacher training. The raising of the standards of the teachers was one of the main aims of the 19th-century educationalists.

Questions

a. What subjects were most teachers capable of teaching?
b. Why could the majority not teach writing?
c. What subjects were 'scarcely ever seen'?
d. Who learned to write?
e. Why did the working-class children not do so?
f. Why did the majority of children not go to school at all?
g. Who was considered 'a far-learned man'?
h. What reasons are given to explain scarcity of: (i) newspapers; (ii) books?

46 The Government and Popular Education, 1839

. . . The zeal for popular education has increased, the Established Church has made great efforts to promote the building of schools, and the National, and British and Foreign School, Societies have . . . endeavoured to stimulate the liberality of the benevolent . . . friends of general Education.

. . . Among the chief defects yet existing may be reckoned the insufficient number of qualified school-masters, the imperfect mode of teaching in . . . the schools, . . . and the want of a Model School which might serve for the example of those . . . anxious to improve their own methods of teaching . . .

. . . I am directed by Her Majesty to desire . . . that your Lordship, with four others . . . should form a board or Committee, for the consideration of all matters affecting the education of the people.

. . . This Board should consist of: the Lord President of the Council; the Lord Privy Seal; the Chancellor of the Exchequer; the Secretary of State for the Home Department; the Master of the Mint.

It is proposed that the Board should be entrusted with the application of any sums which may be voted by Parliament for the purposes of education . . . .

Among the first objects to which any grant may be applied will be the establishment of a Normal [Model] School.

In such a school a body of schoolmasters may be formed, competent to assume the management of similar institutions in all parts of the country. In such a school likewise the best modes of teaching may be introduced, and those who wish to improve the schools of their neighbourhood may have an opportunity of observing their results.

The Board will consider whether it may not be advisable . . . to apply a sum of money annually in aid of the Normal [Model] Schools of the . . . Societies.

Parliamentary Papers, 1839, XLI, pp. 255–7.

Comment

There were many attempts to improve the quality of education in the late 18th and early 19th centuries, and this extract from a letter from Lord John Russell, the Whig politician, to Lord Lansdowne cites some of the difficulties.

The first attempts were made possible by private donations, in keeping with the age of 'self-help'. The two most important educational societies are mentioned in paragraph 1. The societies invited generous and wealthy townsfolk to subscribe for the building of a school, and appealed to them, each year, for contributions for running that school. In 1833 the Government made the first financial contribution to help the two societies.

This document stresses the need for training teachers.

A new feature described in this letter was the setting up of a Government Committee to deal with the now increased grant for education.

Questions

a. Lord Lansdowne wrote of 'zeal for popular education'. What three proofs does he offer to prove his point?

b. What, according to paragraph 2, are the chief defects and weaknesses in the system of education in 1839?

c. How would the setting up of a Training College (Normal or Model school) improve matters?

d. What did the Government propose to do about such a school or college?

e. Who were to serve on the new Board?

f. Is there any evidence in the document that there were already Training Colleges in existence?

g. Write a paragraph on the work of the National and the British and Foreign Societies.

h. What grant did the Government give these societies in: (i) 1833; (ii) 1839?

47 What Schools Should Teach, 1861

... I doubt whether it would be desirable, with a view to the real interests of the peasant boy, to keep him at school till he was 14 or 15 years of age. But it is not possible. We must make up our minds to see the last of him ... at 10 or 11.... It is quite possible to teach a child ... all that is necessary for him to possess ... by the time that he is 10 years old. ... He shall be able to spell correctly the words that he will ordinarily have to use; he shall read a common narrative — the paragraph in the newspaper that he cares to read — with sufficient ease to be a pleasure to himself and to convey information to listeners; if gone to live at a distance from home, he shall write his mother a letter that shall be both legible and intelligible; he knows enough of ciphering to make out, or test the correctness of, a common shop bill; if he hears talk of foreign countries he has some notions as to the part of the habitable globe in which they lie; ... he has acquaintance enough with the Holy Scriptures to follow ... the arguments of a plain ... sermon, and a ... recollection of the truths taught him in his catechism to know what are the duties required of him ...

I have no bright view of the future or the possibilities of an English elementary education floating before my eyes ... If I had ever dreamt ... dreams before, what I have seen in the last six months would have ... for ever dissipated them.

Evidence of Rev. James Fraser to the Newcastle Commission.

Comment

This is an extract from the evidence given to the first Royal Commission on Education, the Newcastle Commission of 1861.

The Commission had appointed ten Assistant Commissioners to examine in detail, for about six months, the educational provisions of a particular district. This is an extract from the evidence of one Assistant Commissioner, the Rev. James Fraser, later Bishop of Manchester.

The majority of children who did go to school, and there was no compulsion for them to do so, left at the age of 11; only 5% of children were at school at the age of 13. Partly because of the need to pay even small fees, partly because of ill health, attendance of those who went to school was poor; few poor children attended full time.

The alleged impossibility of a better system was disproved by the American and Prussian systems (Book II, Section 1).

Questions

a. At what age, according to the Commissioner, should children leave school?

b. What did the Commissioner expect a working-class person to know?

c. 'Education means the 3 r's.' Would the Commissioner have agreed?

d. What did the Commissioner think of English elementary education?

e. Why were British workmen not able to learn the new technical subjects when they left school?

f. Can you see any improvement since 1820 (Document 45)?

g. Compare the subjects taught in the 1860s with those taught in the 1960s.

h. Why had other reforms (Document 35) made educational reform essential?

48 The Education Act, 1870

5. There shall be [in] every school district a sufficient amount of . . . public elementary schools for all the children . . .
6. Where there is an insufficient amount of accommodation, a school Board shall be formed [to] supply such deficiency.
7. (i) It shall not be required that [any child] shall attend . . . any instruction in religious subjects . . .;
   (ii) the time during which [religious] instruction is given shall be either at the beginning or at the end of [the day]. . . .
10. If after six months the Education Department are satisfied that all the accommodation required has not been supplied, the Education Department shall cause a school board to be formed to supply the same . . .
17. Every child attending a school shall pay . . . fees prescribed by the school Board. The Board may . . . remit . . . part of such fee when they are of the opinion that the parent is unable to pay the same (from poverty).
26. If a school Board satisfies the Education Department that, on the ground of poverty, it is expedient to provide a school at which no fees shall be required, the Board may provide such a school . . .
54. Any sum required to meet any deficiency in the school fund shall be paid out of the local rate.
74. Every Board may make byelaws for any of the following purposes; (i) requiring parents of children not less than five years nor more than thirteen years, to cause such children to attend school; provided that any such byelaw shall provide for the exemption of a child if one of Her Majesty's Inspectors certifies that such child has reached a standard of education specified in such byelaw.

Statutes of the Realm, **33 & 34** Victoria, c. **75.**

Comment

The Education Bill, 1870, was introduced by W. E. Forster, who recognised the poor quality of elementary education (Documents 45 and 47). He claimed that this poor quality was the result of the Government not doing enough (an argument used by T. H. Green in Document 36). He proposed a major reform of the educational structure.

He took as his model the Public Health system that Chadwick had devised (Document 15). The central Education Department (Document 46) would continue to help existing schools, but would also supervise the work of the locally elected School Boards which were to be set up by this Act.

Questions

a. When could a School Board be set up?

b. When could the central Education Department insist that one be set up?

c. What did the Act say about: (i) attendance at religious instruction; (ii) the time at which religious instruction was to be given?

d. What does the extract say about fees?

e. Which children could be exempted from paying fees?

f. Was attendance at school compulsory under this Act? What is the importance of 'may' in paragraph 74?

g. The Education Department made grants to schools (Document 46) and the pupils paid fees. Where would the School Boards get any other money they might require?

h. When was elementary education made: (i) compulsory; (ii) free? When was the age limit raised to 14?

Conclusion

In 1750 Britain was predominantly an agricultural country; by 1870 she had become the workshop of the world. In 1750 the majority of the population lived in village communities; by 1870 most of the vastly increased population lived in towns. In 1750 a small group of people dominated the social and political life of the country; by 1870 new classes had emerged, a more democratic political system had evolved. In 1750 there was little effective local government, and the central government played only a small part in the life of the people; by 1870 reformed councils were applying the laws passed by the central government, as *laissez-faire* gave way to the philosophy of communal co-operation.

The Industrial Revolution had brought increased wealth; this was being shared out among a majority of the population, although a large minority remained desperately poor. The State which had begun to tackle the problems of public health was not yet ready to tackle the problem of poverty.

An administrative framework had been created to administer the laws passed in the period; this framework would have to be extended to cope with the remaining social problems. This is the subject matter of Book II. In that book, too, we will see how Britain lost its position as the foremost industrial nation.